Is That Your Child?

Is That Your Child?

Mothers Talk about Rearing Biracial Children

MARION KILSON AND FLORENCE LADD

LEXINGTON BOOKS

A Division of
ROWMAN & LITTLEFIELD PUBLISHERS, INC.
Lanham • Boulder • New York • Toronto • Plymouth, UK

LEXINGTON BOOKS

A division of Rowman & Littlefield Publishers, Inc.
A wholly owned subsidiary of The Rowman & Littlefield Publishing Group, Inc.
4501 Forbes Boulevard, Suite 200
Lanham, MD 20706

Estover Road
Plymouth PL6 7PY
United Kingdom

British Library Cataloguing in Publication Information Available

Library of Congress Cataloging-in-Publication Data

Kilson, Marion, 1936–
  Is that your child? : mothers talk about rearing biracial children / Marion Kilson and
Florence Ladd.
    p. cm.
  Includes bibliographical references and index.
  ISBN-13: 978-0-7391-2763-6 (cloth : alk. paper)
  ISBN-10: 0-7391-2763-2 (cloth : alk. paper)
  ISBN-13: 978-0-7391-2764-3 (pbk. : alk. paper)
  ISBN-10: 0-7391-2764-0 (pbk. : alk. paper)
  ISBN-13: 978-0-7391-3208-1 (electronic)
  ISBN-10: 0-7391-3208-3 (electronic)
  1. Racially mixed children—United States. 2. Child rearing—United States. 3.
Mothers—United States. 4. Motherhood—United States. I. Ladd, Florence. II. Title.
  HQ777.9.K55 2009
  306.84'6—dc22   2008030643

Printed in the United States of America

∞™ The paper used in this publication meets the minimum requirements of American
National Standard for Information Sciences—Permanence of Paper for Printed Library
Materials, ANSI/NISO Z39.48–1992.

For Our Families

Contents

Preface

"Is that your child?" is a question that countless mothers of biracial children in the United States encounter, whether they are African Americans or European Americans, rearing children today or a generation ago, living in the city or in the suburbs, are upper-middle-class or middle-class. In this book we probe mothers' responses to this query as well as their accounts of other challenges and rewards of parenting biracial children.

We began our conversations about parenting biracial children by recounting our own experiences. Marion Kilson, a European American, and Florence Ladd, an African American, became parents of biracial children in the 1960s and 1970s, respectively. Although we and our spouses have been friends for longer than we have been mothers, we had never conversed at length about racial aspects of our parenting experiences until we began this project. Rather, our conversations—like our conversations with

other friends—over the years had focused on professional concerns and cultural interests.

Since we were curious about the commonalities and
differences between our experiences and those of other
black and white women with biracial children, we set out
to interview black mothers whose children's fathers were
white men and white mothers whose children's fathers
were black men. Some of these women were members of our
generation; others were younger. Some women's childrearing days were well behind them; others were rearing
young children or adolescents when we met with them. We
talked to women whom we already knew and to others
whom we first met during our interviews. All are middle-
class or upper-middle-class in socioeconomic status, living
today in the greater Boston area of Massachusetts. All were
generously candid with their recollections and reflections.

As we considered the wealth of information about
these women's biracial parenting experiences, we found
that there were parenting issues that transcended generations and some that were characteristic of only one generation. We discovered that mothers differed in their levels
of race awareness as parents as well as in the importance
that they gave to racial considerations in parenting their
children.

Our book begins with our initial interview of one another, continues with an overview of the challenges and
rewards of rearing biracial children gleaned from semi-
structured interviews with other mothers, presents pro-

files of mothers highlighting distinctive individual biracial parenting experiences, assesses key factors in nurturing confident young biracial Americans, and concludes with a review of lessons learned for successful parenting of biracial children.

We believe that our book makes a unique contribution to the growing body of literature by and about biracial Americans. In the past twenty years biracial Americans like Rebecca Walker, June Cross, Barack Obama, and James McBride have written of their personal experiences and scholars like Kathleen Korgen, Maria Root, and Ruth Frankenberg have explored aspects of the biracial experience.[1] Jane Lazarre and Maureen T. Reddy have written memoirs of their own experiences as mothers of biracial children and Marguerite Wright and Donna Jackson Nakazawa have created biracial parenting guides.[2] To our knowledge, no one has focused on the biracial parenting experiences of a heterogeneous set of black and white mothers of different generations and socioeconomic circumstances as we do in this book.

Our book is made possible only through the generosity of the mothers who shared their stories and insights with us. We wish to acknowledge our gratitude both to those mothers who preferred that we not identify them and to those who allowed us to name them. For their candor and insights, we are grateful to Agnes Bundy-Scanlan, Gwendolyn DuBois Shaw, Marilyn Glater, Jacqueline Goggin, Suzanne Hauck, Hannah Laws Kilson, Bobbie Knable,

Claudia Knight, Brenda M. Kronberg, Renee M. Landers, Mary E. McClain, Cynthia Monteiro, Beverly Morgan-Welch, Florence P. Rawls, and Joan Reitmayer-Debow. We gratefully acknowledge the invaluable counsel of several of our colleagues—George Clement Bond, Peter Gamble, Lindy Hess, and Janie Ward. Finally, we thank and dedicate this book to our families—husbands, children, and grandchildren who have shared our life adventures navigating a complex multiracial world—Bill Harris, Martin Kilson, Jennifer Kilson-Page, Peter Kilson, Hannah Kilson, Michael Ladd, Jacob Kilson Page, Rhiana Kilson Page, Maya Kilson Page, Caila Marion Kilson-Kuchtic, Zuri Helen Kilson-Kuchtic, Ciaran Martin Kilson-Kuchtic, Martin Ladd, John Kuchtic, Fanny Pagniez Ladd, and Phillip Page.

NOTES

1. See Selected References.

2. Other noteworthy contributions to this literature include books by Lise Funderberg, Peggy Gillespie and Gigi Kaesar, Angela Nissei, Claudine Chiawei O'Hearn, and Sharon Rush.

1

The Backstory of *Is That Your Child?*

Listening—just listening. Listening to their expressions about race, listening to what they say about race or incidents that have affected them; preparing them in some way.

On an early spring morning in a sunlit university office in Cambridge, two friends sat down to discuss a hitherto undiscussed but mutually engaging topic. Although Marion Kilson—an anthropologist, graduate school dean, and essayist—and Florence Ladd—psychologist, university administrator, novelist, and poet—had known one another for four decades, sharing many family holidays and celebrations, they had never discussed at length their experiences as mothers of mixed-race children.

Born in New Haven, Connecticut, Marion Kilson, a European American, grew up in the Boston area. She attended independent schools that lacked any racial diversity and had very little ethnic, religious, or socioeconomic heterogeneity. In college she met Martin Kilson, an African American political science graduate student, whom she married three years later in 1959 over the vehement objections of her extended family. Their children were born in the 1960s—Jennifer in 1963, Peter in 1964, and Hannah in 1966. A graduate of Radcliffe College with an M.A. from Stanford University, she received her Ph.D. in social anthropology from Harvard University in 1967.

Florence Ladd was born in Washington, D.C., where she attended racially segregated public schools. She is a graduate of Howard University (B.S.) and the University of Rochester (Ph.D.), with a concentration in social psychology. Her marriage to a high school classmate ended in divorce. In 1969, she married John Ladd, a European American archaeologist. (He, too, had been married previously and had four children.) Their son, Michael, was born in 1970. John Ladd died of a heart attack in 1971. In 1974, Florence met William J. Harris, a European American designer, sculptor, and entrepreneur. He had two children by a previous marriage. He and Florence have co-parented Michael ever since they met; they were wed in 1984. Since then, Florence has counted among her family six stepchildren, all of whom are European American. Michael, her only offspring, is biracial.

Wishing to know more about her children's experience as biracial Americans and to discover how their experiences compared to other biracial Americans of their generation, Marion interviewed young adult biracial Americans across the country in the 1990s. Those interviews led first to an exhibition of photographs and texts, "Claiming Place: Biracial American Portraits," and then in 2001 to a book, *Claiming Place: Biracial Young Adults in the Post–Civil Rights Era.* The exploration of young adults' lives led Marion to questions about the parenting experiences of black and white mothers of biracial children, which she wished to pursue. Florence Ladd agreed to join her in this inquiry. Both Florence's son Michael and Marion's children were well launched in their careers and in establishing their own families when Florence and Marion sat down to their candid conversation about parenting biracial children.

Marion: Florence, when Michael was born, what did you expect his racial identification would be?

Florence: I don't think that I gave much thought to his racial identification. But it was Jeffrey Ladd's interest in his racial identification—Jeffrey [his half-brother] who desperately wanted a black brother—that made me aware of what it meant to his siblings and it made me think about his future and racial identification in infancy. Michael was fairer than Jeffrey had hoped. And I felt that I had let Jeffrey down in some way.

Did I have expectations? Not in the early years.

How about your expectations?

Marion: Well, I was very clear that my children were going to be African American. That was my primary thought about racial identity.

When I was pregnant with Jenny [her eldest child], I was still in graduate school. I was taking a course on African American society and culture. I decided to do a paper on slave revolts for the course, because I wanted to be able to tell my child that African Americans had not accepted slavery docilely.

So I always had the notion that my children didn't have a choice. That didn't mean that they wouldn't be very much involved with my side of the family. But I felt that it was very important that they consider themselves African Americans, because the world was going to view them that way. So an African American identity for my children was always an expectation for me.

Florence: Marion, tell me about incidents or remarks related to race early in the lives of your children and how they and you responded to them.

Marion: Well, the first incident that I remember was when Jenny was about six months old. I was shopping in a supermarket with her. An elderly white woman came up to me and said with hostile disapproval, "Is this your child?" I responded, "Yes, she is my child." That was the first incident that I remember.

When Jenny was five, she began to feel ambivalent about being brown. We were going to Ghana for the summer to do research and I thought, "Oh, wonderful, there she will be in an all-black environment, it will be so affirming, it will be marvelous." It was anything but marvelous, because the cultural cues were different. So she—who in this culture was very gregarious on the street, stopping people, talking to them with great comfort—refused to go out of the house in Ghana unless Martin or I or our babysitter took her out until she established friendships in the neighborhood. That was a good lesson for me about the importance of culture and how culture really transcended race for her in that context.

Jenny probably had more problems with racial issues than either Peter or Hannah at comparable ages, partly because she was relatively shy. When we moved to Lexington, she had real problems in school for the first time. She was called "popcorn head." A boy called her "nigger"; she chased that boy all the way to his home as a way of dealing with that racial slur. I remember calling the school and talking with the principal about the incident and saying, "I'm amazed that we've moved to the suburbs and we've had these problems that we've never had before." The principal was very sympathetic and spoke with the child's mother, who was appalled because this parent was very supportive of Lexington becoming more racially diverse. So Jenny had those experiences and I don't think that Peter or Hannah had the same ones. As an adolescent, Jenny had more ambivalence about her racial identity than Hannah.

What about Michael?

Florence: The early incident that I remember occurred in an upscale Harvard Square culinary store. Michael was three years old and had that huge brown-blondish Afro. And we both overheard two saleswomen talking about us to one another. "He must be adopted," one of them said. "Why would she have adopted *him*?" the other one said. And Michael heard the remarks and said, "Let's get out of this store." I don't know that we talked about what we had heard. I found it hurtful and I'm not sure that I had a formulation for him and didn't know just how he had interpreted the incident. I waited for him to say something about it. It passed. I don't know if he remembers it. I still remember the incident very vividly.

At Shady Hill School when he was maybe about second grade, he was called "nigger" by two boys. His teacher reported that he responded, "I'm not a nigger! I'm African American, I'm white American, I'm Native American, I'm all American!" And the teacher reported it was a healthy response.

I was up in arms and spent some time in the principal's office talking about the incident, which the principal was not eager to take up, as "these things did not happen at Shady Hill." In any case, we engaged—with the teacher's assistance—the parents of the two other children and it was talked through as an issue in class. I think that was a turning point for Michael.

Beyond that it was out of my hands. He went to boarding school and I don't know what happened after eighth grade. I think around that time race and sports began to have some influence. That he was not good in basketball was an issue for him. I think that he felt he would have been more credibly black if he had been good at basketball. He played all the kinds of sports that Shady Hill encouraged—lacrosse, soccer, hockey. But he really wanted to be good at basketball.

Marion: Well, all three of my kids played basketball, among other things.

Who else played important roles in Michael's racial identity development besides you?

Florence: Michael's identity is black. I think our housekeeper and her family played an important role in that. And in some ways his half-siblings did, especially Jeffrey, who has always posed questions about race to both of us. Jeffrey's curiosity about race has been overt and he has sometimes asked the rude questions. I don't know when he began talking to Michael about race, but it's been part of their dialogue. I think if there's been some sharpening of racial identity, Jeffrey contributed to that. Teachers, especially his first teacher—she was just very affirming about race and wonderful with Michael; I think she was the only black teacher that he had at Shady Hill.

Marion: To what extent do you and Bill hold similar or divergent views about childrearing, especially with respect to racial identity?

Florence: Bill initially used to function in a color-blind way. He didn't see differences. Michael and Bill have had serious discussions about race, with Michael pointing out the differences and injustices and inequities. I would say that Bill and I—now that childrearing is over—are on the same page and our views are congruent. If anything he has become blacker than both Michael and me.

Marion: How did relationships with your own and John Ladd's and Bill's families impact Michael's racial identity development?

Florence: On the Ladd side, Michael has been greatly cherished not only by Jeffrey, for reasons that have nothing to do with race, but by all the kids. He's the youngest and truly their brother; they never say "half-brother"—"my brother." And Helen Ladd [John's first wife] took an interest in Michael from the beginning; Michael when he was about four began referring to her as his "half-mother." And I tried to explain that that wasn't a term and his reasoning was, "Well, if they're my half-brothers and -sisters, she's my half-mother."

And what about you?

Marion: Who played an important role in my kids' racial identity development? Well, obviously Martin played a very very important role—particularly in his being very positive about being black, but also in taking no truck with any racial aspersions being cast on them.

And I think where we differed is that his response was to encourage them to have a physical response to racial incidents, whereas I would have encouraged them to talk it out. But I felt as though he had more experience with race than I did, so I deferred to him. But when they were small and ran into those "popcorn head" kinds of incidents, he certainly told them to respond physically. So that was important.

I don't think that our babysitter was important in their racial identity development at a verbal level; it was important for me that she was black. Certainly in terms of their general development, my aunt was enormously important, as somebody of a different race who was very loving toward them and had a lot to do with nurturing them.

For many summers one or another of Martin's nieces or nephews stayed with us and I think the way in which we stayed in touch with that side of the family in general was important, because it taught the kids about class as well as being partly a racial experience. As for Peter, the relationship with Martin's nephew, Tom, is very significant; in some ways I think Tom is his big brother. Tom remembers our children presenting a united front; if you did anything to one of them, the other two would respond. So I think those cousins were important in the development of our children's understanding, probably subliminally, of race. And certainly race is constantly being talked about in our house—a major topic of conversation, even if it is not directly aimed at identity issues.

Florence: I think Michael refers to our housekeeper's children as "cousins." On our trips to Washington, there were no cousins his age. My other cousins were in North Carolina or Virginia, and Michael didn't get acquainted with them until later.

Marion, describe your extended family and friendship circles.

Marion: I would say that we've always had a diverse extended family and diverse friendship circles. Although it's interesting to me that in graduate school and early professional life, we had more Jewish and Asian friends than we have now. But when the kids were growing up, there was a lot of diversity among our friends.

Florence: Certainly we've had more white friends than black—just by virtue of where we live—our colleagues.

When Michael was twelve, I signed on for a West African trip through the Howard Alumni Association, because I wanted him to see a range of black professionals. There were two busloads of us. He had a terrific time; he often arranged to be on a different bus. One regret is not keeping in touch with all those people for an extended period of time—we exchanged Christmas cards for a couple of years but that was it.

Marion: Well, that suggests an experience that I had forgotten—summer camp. I sent all three of them one summer to a settlement house camp, which meant that they were with primarily black kids, and I think that was a good experience. Peter had only one other camp experience—when he worked one summer as a dishwasher. And Jenny had a couple of years of additional experience in a predominantly white camp where she was a junior counselor. But Hannah became a camp junkie; she went to camp all through college. She ended up for many years at Agassiz Village, which is a fascinatingly diverse place. It's diverse in terms of physical ability. For many summers she was taking care of physically disabled kids. And it's economically very diverse—upper-middle-class kids and low income. And racially very diverse. So it's an interesting place. She loved camp. At Agassiz Village she was always a staff member—she started when she was a junior in high school and continued all through college. So that was another context where race was an important factor.

Hannah has commented how it was strange to her that she always had a boyfriend in camp but she didn't have a boyfriend in Lexington, whereas Jenny always had a boyfriend in Lexington who was white. One of the traumatic things for Hannah, which I didn't fully realize at the time, was that in high school she had great close friendships with boys but she never had a dating relationship. That her friends could not take the next step was difficult for her.

Florence Ladd and Her Family, June 2008; photo credit: Todd Lee

Marion Kilson and Her Family, June 2008

Florence: The summer that Michael was eleven, I rented a house on Martha's Vineyard. That summer he had the experience of seeing other boys who looked like him. I remember looking out on the beach one day and I didn't know which one was Michael. There were about seven boys—the same color hair. I don't know how he remembers that experience, but I remember it as being very important to him.

Marion: That there were other people who were like him.

Florence: Exactly, exactly.

How about religious institutions?

Marion: We aren't involved in religious institutions. Martin used to make us all go to the local community church in the summer for a while. And in terms of his family, the church in Ambler, his hometown, is important, so we've been there.

Florence: We used to go to Friends Meeting—entirely white. When we went to Washington, we went to Second Baptist Church—his only black church experience as far as I know—exhilarating in some way.

Marion: I think the Ambler church probably was culturally important. One of Martin's sisters was quite a well known gospel singer, so they had that kind of experience.

Florence: In your family photo album, is one side of the family dominant?

Marion: I suppose that my side of the family is dominant. My side of the family has generations of pictures, whereas there's one picture of Martin's early childhood and a few of his boyhood. But in terms of what we've created, it's probably pretty evenly balanced. And it reflects the fact that we've mainly lived around here.

How about your family album?

Florence: It's populated with a lot of Ladds, as many of the occasions that call for cameras were birthday parties, graduations, ceremonial occasions that we celebrated with Ladds.

Marion: But that's also partly a reflection of the fact that you don't have a lot of family. If you had five siblings, it would be different. Right?

Florence: Exactly.

Marion: Florence, as a parent, what do you think are key considerations in rearing biracial children?

Florence: Listening—just listening. Listening to their expressions about race; listening to what they say about race or incidents that have affected them; preparing them in some way. I think of it as giving them some armor—protective armor, which I felt that I had growing up in a black community, in black schools with just everybody in authority being black—the teachers, the principal, the dentist, the lawyer, the minister—the entire range of people. And I think I've told Michael about my growing up that way. I was certainly more hurt by that name-calling incident at Shady Hill than he was. His response was more constructive and self-assured. I heard it in a way that was painful. Key considerations—exposing them to a lot of situations that affirm their black identity.

Marion: I think that's really important and I think that the choice of books and of cultural events is significant. Again, when our kids were small, you were more hard-pressed to find books with black characters than you are now. I remember a friend giving my children a book, *Black is Beautiful,* which was great, because there weren't very many books like that.

Florence: Ezra Jack Keats—those books.

Marion: Yes, I adored them—*Snowy Day.* . . .

Florence: The books are important. Museum experiences, musical events—*Black Nativity*—I don't know how many times one needs to see it, but that was one event I could count on.

Marion: That's still part of our Christmas ritual.

Florence: What statements, messages, or principles did you offer with respect to race?

Marion: I think that we tried to offer a very positive affirming one. Certainly black achievement was important in general. And I think that the exposure, as we've been discussing, to people whom we knew. I don't know what else to say about that issue except to affirm and to comment critically on the world around us.

Florence: I think that I literally said to Michael from time to time, "You have a certain privilege or responsibility, because you have access to both worlds—black and white." I think at first I used to say, "You can't take sides, because part of your family is white," when he was clearly black-identified and angry. And I pulled back from that, because he had taken sides, but I continued to remind him that he had the potential to be a mediator or someone who could see both sides of racial issues and contribute to reconciliation.

Marion: I don't think I was that idealistic, because again it comes back to the very first question about expectations of racial identification.

Florence: That kind of idealism was a shortcoming.

Marion: A shortcoming that we had was a lack of sensitivity to residence. We moved out of Cambridge because of the cost, because we wanted a good public school system, and because we didn't want our kids exposed to the Harvard Square culture. But probably we should have been more sensitive—maybe we shouldn't have lived in Cambridge, but we ought to have lived in a more racially mixed area. I think that would have been helpful. I didn't realize it fully at the time. But clearly all our kids have chosen to live in the city, because they like to see visual diversity. So I think that was a shortcoming.

Another shortcoming gets back to your point about listening, because one can miss key times. I remember when Jenny was probably twelve. I was in the midst of doing something on a Saturday morning and she said to me, "You're white and Dad's black and we're black. Is that right?" Obviously that was a really important conversation to begin to have and I just didn't have it. I just said to her, "Yes, that's right." We just went on with whatever we were doing, but it was terrible to have missed that moment.

But I don't think that any of my children has been truly angry about race in the way that Michael was angry. I think that they, as Michael does, function well in a bicultural, biracial world; I think that they are basically comfortable with all kinds of people and that's good. And I think that comfort comes out of their own initial experiences.

Florence: I regret now not having made more of an effort to go to visit my cousins. The cousins of my generation on my mother's side have grandchildren. Michael found a cousin in New York and saw a lot of him; they developed a close friendship. They both were interested in knowing each other, hanging out together, spending a lot of social time together, but I should have made that happen. It's not a huge regret, but it's a regret.

Marion: How do you assess Michael's perspective on race in his life today?

Florence: Race is very important to Michael. In another time, he would have been called a "race man." He would have founded a movement and given himself to that. That he is using his art form to convey a lot of racial and political messages is his way of doing it now. I don't think he is as angry as he used to be. I think he's come to terms with some things about this country and its possibilities. I feel this country has let him down, that he wants to move to France.

Marion: Does he see this as a long-term move?

Florence: I think so. In part because of his relationship with Fanny, his fiancée, who is biracial. He has said that he has felt more comfortable with her than he has ever felt in any other relationship. I don't think that that has to do with race. I think some of it has to do with Fanny's maturity and his. But he talks about it in terms of lifestyle. Her apartment in some ways reminds him of our house. There are some things that he resonates with that are good for him. I hope that he will find the time to put on paper some of the inspired things that he says about race, things that don't make their way into poems or into his rap. He has a narrative that I think is a kind of resolution for him about race.

Marion: I think for all my kids race is very important. Hannah perceives herself in a biracial marriage and that the children are biracial. Certainly all of them work in and around racial issues in their work.

Peter, after several years in France, came back and spent ten years working with inner-city kids in a variety of ways. He continues to tutor some black kids and his spare time activities are in and around the black experience.

For Jenny it was important to move to Brookline so that her kids would have a more affirming racial experience. It turns out that the school that they attend isn't too different from some of the schools that they went to in Lexington. She's put a lot of effort into making the Boston kids in the METCO program feel comfortable in the school, making sure that they are well looked after and getting people to be much more aware of diversity issues in the school—in fact, in the whole Brookline school system.[1] And then in her higher education work that links Boston public schools and colleges race is clearly important.

And race is important for Hannah. In the long run her real interest is in community development. Whether she will ever really be able to give up the corporate law rat race is a question, but her *pro bono* work is in and around affordable housing and also the boards on which she sits relate to that.

So for all three of them I think race is very important and for the girls being sure that their children have good affirming racial experiences.

Florence: How did the racial identity development of your children compare?

Marion: I think the fact that they're all the same color— they have all commented on that as being something that made their experiences more alike. Obviously temperament is very important. I think Jenny and Peter probably had more difficult times than Hannah had, because she's so verbally assertive. And birth order is important. Hannah's perception is that the other two paved the way for her.

Florence: In what ways would you say that your husband's account of these issues would differ from yours?

Marion: He would be much less tuned in to the emotional side, but I don't think he'd have a different view.

Florence: I think Bill would have a totally different interpretation—totally unrelated to the reality of things.

Marion: That's interesting. Do you want to elaborate on that comment?

Florence: Well, I just think Bill's constructed a story about Michael's growing up and his [Bill's] coming into our lives—it's not so much about race, but rather on how people value his performance and what he has to offer.

Marion: Florence, how do you think that your experience as a parent of a biracial child differs from that of your parents' generation or of Michael's generation?

Florence: That's a difficult question.

Marion: I perceive that for our children, they didn't have a public choice about racial identity, whereas for our children's generation, their children have a choice about affirming all of their identities. I think that's a big difference in terms of expectations; maybe it makes the situation more complicated, but I think that's a big difference.

Florence: I think in terms of numbers. There are many more biracial children now and it is somehow fashionable. If you look at fashion models, Benetton ads, the GAP figures.

Marion: One of the people whom I interviewed for my study of biracial young adults was a model. She talked about how she was successful or not as a model depending on what was "in." Sometimes she was too dark or too light or whatever. Visually there are many more cues to diversity. It's a much more generally affirming culture—structurally, things may not have changed a whole lot.

Florence Ladd and Marion Kilson concluded their conversation with thoughts about how their experiences might differ from others of their generation and of the next generation and how to reach these mothers of biracial children to explore their experiences of biracial mothering. They decided to begin by talking with women whom they knew. From them they learned of others. Ultimately they interviewed twenty-one mothers of biracial offspring in the greater Boston area. Their childrearing years spanned nearly half a century.

NOTE

1. METCO, the acronym for the state-funded Metropolitan Council for Educational Opportunity in Massachusetts, seeks to provide diversity in public education by enabling selected Boston and Springfield students to attend schools in suburban communities.

2

Challenges and Rewards for Mothers of Biracial Children

People are always trying to figure out the mystery of biracial children. . . . Twenty-five years ago people were staring. . . . They are still staring, but I think it's less strange for people. So they don't stare with the same kind of confusion on their faces.

BACKGROUND

Although their parents, aunts, and uncles may have discouraged or disapproved of their interracial marriages and expressed reservations about prospects for their biracial children, most of the mothers queried entered into parenting with a measure of preparedness for the race-related challenges they were likely to encounter. Indeed, some of the mothers of young children view the years ahead with optimism and a spirit of adventure. They cite the frequent appearance of biracial actors and models in the broadcast and print media as evidence of the fashionable value of blended looks. Being biracial is currently hip, one young mother stated: "In American society it's 'in' to be mixed now in a way that it wasn't 'in' in the sixties. It's a very hip thing."

In the United States interracial marriages between blacks and whites have increased from 51,000 in 1960 to 403,000 in 2006. Today approximately one-third of such marriages are between a black woman and a white man and two-thirds between a black man and a white woman.[1] Yet the percentage of such marriages is small among married black and white Americans, for 6.6 percent of married black men and 2.8 percent of married black women have a white spouse, while 0.2 percent white males and 0.5 percent of white females have a black spouse.[2] Moreover, black/white intermarriage numbers are consistently lower than those for marriages between other racial groups.[3]

Another noteworthy trend is that the socioeconomic attributes of interracial partners have changed. Whereas during the first half of the twentieth century most marriages between African Americans and European Americans were between individuals of lower socioeconomic status, during the second half of the century and into the twenty-first century, most interracial marriages have been between middle- and upper-middle-class people with respect to education and income.[4] The socioeconomic attributes of the black and white mothers to whom we talked mirror these national trends, for all are middle- and upper-middle-class.[5]

The parenting experiences of our cohort of black and white mothers span nearly five decades. In public settings, when observed with their biracial offspring, over five decades people still stare. Perhaps it is not an expression of confusion—or even hostility; rather, it may be mere curiosity about how they have become a family or how they have managed to remain united in a society that has not readily accepted interracial and intercultural intimacy.

Curious about the varieties of mothering biracial children, we wanted to know about mothers' childrearing goals and how they influenced the racial identity of their offspring. Mothers of biracial children want for their children what all mothers want; they want to nurture secure, confident individuals with the ability to experience a sense of accomplishment as they develop and mature.

We have clustered our black and white mothers into five groups according to their children's ages and their levels of race awareness or the extent to which race is salient in their parenting. We have found that black and white women whose children are grown and have left home for the world of work and the creation of their own families confronted somewhat different parenting issues than women whose children are young and still at home. For white mothers, high awareness of racial issues has been acquired through observation, empathy, and personal encounters. Family histories and lifelong racial vigilance heightened the awareness of most, but not all, black mothers. Our fifth category is comprised of mothers, black and white, who appear to avoid race as a significant consideration in nurturing their chil-

Table 1.   Summary: Some Sociological Attributes of Mothers[1]

	Black	White
Education		
High School Graduate	0	1
Bachelor's Degree	4	2
Master's Degree	1	3
JD	5	0
PhD	2	3
Occupation		
Attorney	3	0
College/University Administrator	2	1
College/University Faculty Member	2	2
Consultant	2	2
Homemaker	1	0
Non-profit Organization Administrator	2	3
Nurse	0	1
Marital Status		
Single	0	1
Married	11	7
Divorced	1	1
Residence		
Urban	9	6
Suburban	3	2
Rural	0	1
Children's Status*		
Child	8	3
Adult	5	7

*One white woman and one black woman have children with adult and child statuses.

1. See Appendix II for greater detail about mothers' sociological attributes.

dren toward adulthood. While we have found that each of these groups of mothers displays certain distinctive attributes, common experiences cut across generation and race.

RACIALLY AWARE BLACK MOTHERS WITH OLDER CHILDREN

The racially aware black mothers of children who are grown and have left home to establish their adult lives with whom we talked are professional women. They include administrators and professors as well as entrepreneurs. They live in Boston and its inner suburbs with their spouses—a disproportionate number of whom are Jewish. As they recalled their parenting experiences, they emphasized major societal issues and remembered significant incidents rather than daily challenges. They talked of their efforts to encourage black identities in their children and their regrets for belatedly hearing their children's untold stories. Some spoke of being welcomed by their in-laws, others of having received lifelong rejection from them. They anticipate that their grandchildren will inhabit a more multicultural world than the one in which their children grew up.

Encouraging Black Identities

With few exceptions these black mothers of biracial children anticipated that their children would be perceived as African Americans and that their identities would be black. As one mother said, "Because the world would see him in that way and he needed to be able to face the world as black." All have encouraged their children to appreciate African American culture through family relationships, family friendships, and cultural experiences. Today their children identify themselves as "black" or "biracial."

Moreover, these women have had their understanding about racial identity issues enhanced by dialogues with their children. While some of their young adult children consider themselves "black" today, others self-identify as "biracial." One woman's son joined a biracial student group at his college, saying "This is something that you and Dad will never know, because you are not biracial. This is something that the black person cannot know about and the white person cannot know about."

While these African American women encouraged their children to self-identify as "black" and to appreciate African American culture and history, they also promoted their children's awareness of their biracial heritage and its implications. One mother created scrapbooks of both her husband's family history and her own. Another recalled instructing her son in the realities of his racial identity, "You are biracial; you cannot take sides." As a second-grader, one child responded to being called a "nigger" by saying "I am not a nigger; I am African American, I am white American, I am Indian American; I am *all* American!"

Although their children have a nuanced understanding of their racial identity, the world does not always perceive them as "black" or "biracial." Strangers view them as persons of color, but not necessarily "black" and "biracial." A Haitian taxi driver may identify them as Dominican, an Indian restaurateur as Indian, a Latino grocer as Hispanic. Thus, whatever their self-perceptions, their appearance is racially ambiguous to strangers. While many biracial young adults are viewed as racially ambiguous, some are identified by others as African American, and some are presumed to be white.

Discovering Untold Stories

Looking back, these black mothers recalled racial incidents that they and their children encountered and stated that often they learned about their children's experiences long after the events occurred. They recalled their young children being the targets of racial slurs from schoolmates. One woman remembered that all the white children in her son's class were invited to a birthday party and he was not; another that her teenage son was followed in a music store and asked to leave; and another that she heard store clerks discussing whether or not she had adopted her fair-skinned son. Although children, in their early years, seem to have shared their racist experiences with their parents as young children, they often did not speak of such encounters as adolescents. Long after the occurrence of a racist incident, a child might reveal it to his parents. Such reticence stemmed both from the child's sense that one should handle the situation on one's own and from the wish to protect parents' sensibilities. As one woman said about a recent conversation concerning the past with her adult daughter, "It was clear that she was trying to protect me from being—in retrospect—hurt about things that had been hurtful to her." Most of these women considered that they had only partial knowledge of their maturing children's problematic racial experiences.

Building Connections

These mothers described household traditions built on different religious practices and cosmopolitan friendships with people of different races and cultures. While some women have relied on rich extended family relationships, others have had little, if any, contact with their husbands' families. In fact, one woman who has had close connections with her husband's older sons and daughters regretted that she had not had time to establish deeper relationships with her own cousins who live in southern states.

Yet several women who are married to Jewish men recounted that they had very little connection with their husband's parents and siblings. One woman had never met her parents-in- law and only became acquainted with a brother-in-law after the parents' deaths; another husband's parents refused to attend his wedding and to establish contact with his family. In response to these rejections, these women and their families have derived emotional warmth and support from African American in-laws and from close friends who have become adopted family members. Despite rejection by their Jewish relatives, these women celebrate both Christian and Jewish holiday traditions.

Looking to the Future

As these women looked back on their biracial child-rearing experiences, they regretted not having had more extended conversations about racial identity with their children. In retrospect they wondered how their racial experience as monoracial black people might differ from their children's. Some also lamented the dearth of information about biraciality available to them as young mothers in the 1960s and 1970s. As they looked toward the future, these women envisaged that more people would be building biracial families—not just black and white, but with "more permutations."

Summing Up

Our conversations with racially aware black women of older children emphasized their efforts to protect their racially ambiguous children with a strong African American identity and cultural awareness while fostering an appreciation of their children's paternal heritage. They also described their efforts to build friendship networks across racial and cultural lines, especially if they experienced rejection by their husbands' families.

These women often acknowledged that as their children grew into adolescence they no longer heard about racial affronts that their children might have encountered. A number of these women used their anticipated conversations with us to explore these hitherto untold stories with their adult children. They recognized that younger mothers of biracial children have potential support systems that were unavailable to them a generation ago and they expect that biracial families will continue to increase in an increasingly racially diverse American society.

RACIALLY AWARE WHITE WOMEN WITH OLDER CHILDREN

Racially aware white women with older children have had more eclectic experiences with race than their black counterparts. Some of the women with whom we talked bore biracial children in the 1960s, some in the mid-1980s, and most in the 1970s. Some have reared not only their own biracial children but also their African American husbands' biracial children from previous marriages. Some are no longer married to the fathers of their children. Today all are professionally engaged; some have experienced considerable socioeconomic advancement through their careers. Some have had work that has taken them and their families across the United States and abroad; others have lived in isolated rural communities as well as inner cities; others have spent their adult lives in affluent suburban communities. The diversity of their children's ages, of their residential experiences, and of their work histories mirrors the eclectic nature of their biracial parenting experiences.

Experiencing Racial Rejection

With few exceptions, these white mothers of older children encountered strong opposition from their natal families to their marriages to African American men. In some instances families were reconciled to the marriage before the wedding, in others only after the birth of children, and in others only after the death of the rejecting parent. One woman recounted how after her divorce from her African American husband, her parents had journeyed from their mid-Atlantic suburban home to her inner-city Boston apartment with an ultimatum: either give up her biracial children or give up her family. She opted to give up her family, only reuniting with her father and siblings after her mother's burial a decade later. The reasons for such familial rejection range from fear of stigmatization for the white family with a black in-law to concern for the social marginalization of the biracial couple. While in most cases relationships between these women and their white relatives were reestablished after a time, in many instances a certain "wariness" persisted, as one woman observed: "On the surface there was peace."

While black family members tended to be initially more accepting of interracial marriages than white family members, some women experienced racial rejection from

their husband's relatives. In several instances the husband's mother opposed her son's marriage—sometimes
on racial grounds, sometimes on religious grounds. One
woman commented that her children had had much more
contact with her white family than with her husband's
black family. She said, "I would say that [my husband's]
family—many of them are racist and have had real issues
with me." Several women, however, emphasized the strong
supportive role that black family members played in the
lives of their biracial families.

Just as many of these women have encountered opposition to their interracial marriages from both white and
black family members, so many have experienced racial
prejudice in their social networks. Several women commented that most of their family friends are either white
or biracial couples, and that they did not feel "total acceptance in black circles." One woman said: "My friends
are all multiethnic and multiracial—I have black friends
and I have white friends . . . and I have Chinese friends. I
wouldn't say that it was a conscious effort—it was more
situational. It was a situation that I put myself and my
family in that we developed these friendships."

Promoting Biracial Identity and Self-Assurance

Although several mothers of older children said that
before their first child was born, they were more concerned with the baby's well-being or gender issues than
with racial identity, most considered that their offspring
would self-identify as African American or biracial. Dur-

ing their children's growing-up years these mothers, in concert with their husbands and other caregivers, sought to ensure that their children became self-assured and self-confident biracial people. They discussed the implications of racial incidents with their children as they occurred. They provided affirming multicultural experiences and environments for their children, and they advocated for them in schools and on the playground.

Without exception, these women have had their relationships with their children challenged. One woman recalled going to a car rental agency with one of her children; the agent said, "Oh, I see you've taken in foster children. That's a good thing to do." To which she responded, "No, this is my daughter." Another remembered how administrators at her daughter's school had tried to insist that she go to a meeting of white parents rather than with her husband to one of black parents. She, however, successfully argued that she belonged at the black parents' meeting "because I was there representing my black daughter and her concerns and her needs." Often these women have encountered the inability of people in public settings to see relationship beyond color.

When their children were young, these mothers recall interpreting racial incidents and advocating for their children's well-being. These women are well aware that as their children matured, they shared less of their experiences of race with their mothers. These untold stories, however, were recounted years later. One woman spoke of her biracial daughter's recent recollection of sitting in a restaurant with her mother and a white girl and overhearing a child ask her mother, "Why is that black girl sitting over there with those white people?" At the time the eight-year-old said nothing, but now, as a teacher, the young biracial woman "tells kids when things happen [to you], say something."

Assessing their accomplishments as parents, these mothers of adult biracial children are pleased that their children are comfortable in both the worlds that their parents brought to their marriages. Their children think more comprehensively about social issues than many of their peers. Some who live in the suburbs wish that they might have given their children more exposure to other children of color through choosing diverse neighborhoods and schools. Some who are alienated from their families wish that their children might have known their families better, and some regret that they have been too protective of their children. On balance, however, these women were proud of their children's accomplishments and their own roles in fostering them. Some acknowledged the profound impact on themselves of their experiences as mothers of biracial children. As one woman said: "I am the person I am because of my marriage and my motherhood and that is related to the fact that I am the mother of biracial children."

Summing Up

Most of the racially aware white women with older children with whom we talked encountered strong opposition to their interracial marriages from their natal families and many perceived that some African Americans resented their marriages to black men. They, like other mothers of biracial children, recounted experiencing painful challenges to their maternal relationship to their children from strangers. These mothers emphasized their endeavors to ensure their children's development as self-assured cosmopolitan biracial people and their pride in its achievement.

RACIALLY AWARE BLACK MOTHERS WITH YOUNG CHILDREN AT HOME

Black mothers who are actively parenting children include both stay-at-home moms and professional working mothers, both suburban and urban dwellers, and both mothers of teenagers and mothers of preschoolers. While their personal life stories are quite different and their perspectives on race also vary, all these women share the perception that race matters in their lives and in the lives of their children. Indeed, three common themes emerge from their reflections on being mothers of biracial children: the fluidity of racial identity, the challenges of biracial parenting, and the building of their children's positive racial identities.

Fluidity of Racial Identity

There is an emerging perception in the United States that racial categories are fluid rather than fixed and immutable. Biracial people can have a choice in how they identify themselves. They may identify themselves monoracially or biracially. Moreover, children's choices may differ from those of their parents. One mother of preschool children expressed the hope that her children would embrace both their father's heritage and her own—that they would identify themselves both as people of color and as white people. Another mother anticipated that her child would consider herself African American in recognition of her proud heritage of black achievement. Her daughter, however, considers herself to be "black and white," preferring this descriptive identification to "biracial." She, however, also thinks that "African American," when considered inclusively to encompass Native Americans and European Americans as well as people of African descent, is an appropriate racial identification. Yet another child variously identifies herself as "biracial" or as "African American, German, and Jewish." A generation ago it would be unlikely that parents would consider that their biracial children could identify themselves or be identified by others as anything but "black."

Encountering Biracial Parenting Challenges

These mothers recognize that their children's experiences and identity are shaped by how others perceive them racially. Such perceptions lead to some of the important challenges of parenting biracial children. Among the most significant biracial parenting challenges today are encountering white blindness, combating racial stereotypes, and confronting overt racism.

Without exception black mothers of biracial children have encountered white blindness. In its most blatant form, white blindness is the inability of whites to perceive the relationship between a darker mother and her lighter child. One black mother had someone else's baby brought to her by a hospital nurse, because the nurse presumed that a blond infant could not be the offspring of a light-skinned black woman. Others have had the experience of being mistaken for their children's nannies by strangers. Teachers and daycare providers initially may fail to perceive the connection between mother and child. Black mothers related such encounters and acknowledged the painful experience of having their relationship with their children challenged or negated.

Black mothers of light-skinned biracial children also are aware that when their children are in public places with their white fathers, they may be perceived as white. Their husbands notice the differential response from strangers that they and their children receive in the absence of their wives.

Black mothers also noted that they did not encounter relational blindness from people of color. One recalled how at a party when she walked into a room of African American strangers where her children had been playing, the strangers immediately made the connection between her and the children—"They look just like you!" Through their life experiences with a greater range of human color permutations—often in their own families—people of color acquire the ability to see beyond color to other physical clues of relationships.

White blindness represents a form of racism, for it exemplifies "white privilege" in contemporary society in the United States.[6] Whites are privileged in that they do not need to have an awareness of the complex human diversity of society in the United States. Even today when biraciality is commercially "in" and Americans are generally more sophisticated about racial matters than a generation ago, many white Americans not only are blind to biraciality but also feel comfortable expressing their misperceptions of racial identities and relationships. Such responses might be attributed to denial or to resorting to conventional racial categories.

Black mothers of biracial children are frequently exposed to racial stereotypes of themselves and their children in public places. One mother, who is a successful corporate lawyer, reported that when she went with her infant for a pediatric appointment, the receptionist failed to ask her for a customary co-payment. The mother later realized that the receptionist assumed that she was on welfare and since welfare clients do not pay co-payments, the receptionist did not request one. After the child's appointment, the mother again approached the receptionist saying that she wished to make her co-payment rather than be billed for it. She added that in the future, the receptionist should ask how a person plans to pay for a medical service and not assume that a person of color is on welfare. Another mother recounted going into a stationery store with her young daughter and inquiring about an expensive pen. Assuming that she would be unable to pay for such a pen, the clerk immediately began asking whether or not the mother was aware of the cost of the pen. She was told that the store did not carry the pen, because of its cost. The mother chastised the clerk for her presumption about her inability to purchase such an expensive pen. Yet another black mother, who had worked in a department store during college, noted being followed by an undercover security agent in a local store and pointed the agent out to her daughter. Such racial profiling of black mothers reveals the micro-inequities that they and their children frequently encounter, experiences that these children rarely encounter when accompanying their white fathers in public places.

Black mothers variously respond to such experiences. Depending on their personalities or the situation, they may directly confront the situation as the lawyer with the receptionist and the pen purchaser with the clerk. Alternatively, they may indirectly handle it by taking pains to insure that they demonstrate by having goods packaged that they have paid for an item. Mothers are mindful that how they handle such situations constitutes a learning experience for their children, in which they intend to model courteous but forceful responses to racial stereotyping.

Confronting Overt Racism

Some mothers addressed children's reports of humiliating racist episodes in school, on a playground, or at a neighbor's house. One black mother recounted that her third-grade daughter came home from school upset, because a white child in her class was taunting her with racial slurs and preventing her from using her locker. The third-grader was very concerned that whatever action her parents took, she not be portrayed as a "victim" to her classmates. The following morning the mother and her husband went to speak with the teacher about their child's experience and to insist that the issue be addressed directly and effectively. The teacher took immediate action to stop the child's racial harassment while preserving her anonymity. Such supportive parental intervention in confronting children's racist experiences contributes to building positive racial identities in biracial children and demonstrates to them how to assert and defend themselves.

These black mothers, currently engaged in parenting, make conscious choices to build positive racial identities in their children. They consider where they choose to live, select appropriate schools for their children and opt for activities that enhance their children's self-worth. In conversations with their children, they describe people with reference to relevant attributes. They attempt to create an environment in which their children feel free to express their experiences and feelings. In short, they consider the issues that all thoughtful parents consider but with particular attention to their racial salience.

While these black mothers recognize the importance of a multiracial environment for their children, only a few live in multiracial neighborhoods. Most of the women with whom we talked live in predominantly white neighborhoods. One mother and her husband, however, consciously chose a Boston neighborhood where they could be comfortable as a biracial couple and where their children "wouldn't have the experience of thinking that their family structure or their parents were odd." All the mothers interviewed seek to build positive racial identities in their children by providing positive role models through books and media choices, by exposing them to a circle of racially diverse friends, by involving children in activities with other multiracial children, by choosing multiracial caregivers and schools, and sometimes by joining multicultural family support groups. One mother said that she and her husband consciously describe people's race and ethnicity so that her children will learn that racial differences are normal and descriptive of people.

Creating an environment where children can talk openly and comfortably about their racial experiences and the racial conundrums that they confront is a widely shared goal for racially conscious black mothers of biracial children. As one mother said: "Just because kids do not speak of racial issues, does not mean that everything is fine." Another mother said that she wished she had discussed race more with her children, who as teenagers seem confused about their racial identity. Most of the women with whom we talked seem to realize discussions about race are important. Moreover, one woman summarized the unique value of mothering a biracial child with these words: "I think that this wonderful adventure that we deliberately engaged in has sought to make us better people and whether or not we actually achieve that is another thing, but I think . . . [biracial parenting] has all the potential for making us better parents, better human beings, if we open our hearts to it."

Summing Up

These racially aware black women with young children at home experience the challenges and rewards of rearing biracial children in their daily lives. They confront the challenges that white blindness, racial stereotypes, and racial discrimination create for them as women of color and as parents of biracial children. They also experience the rewards of assisting their children to develop as self-confident biracial Americans in a society that increasingly acknowledges their existence. In 2000, the United States Census—the public arbiter of racial classifications in the United States—for the first time allowed Americans to select more than one racial category to identify themselves. 6.8 million people (2.4 percent) selected that option in 2000. Although fewer selected that option in the 2005 Census Bureau's American Community Survey, 1,290,000 mixed-race individuals chose to identify themselves as black *and* white.[7] Mothers of young biracial children can anticipate a time when society in the United States will acknowledge and affirm their children.

RACIALLY AWARE WHITE MOTHERS WITH CHILDREN AT HOME

The white mothers with whom we talked who are actively parenting children include mothers of primary school students and mothers of high school and college students. They include single mothers and mothers living with their husbands and children. All are professional working women living in urban, suburban, or rural settings. All have given considerable thought to fostering their children's identities as persons of color, though they acknowledge their naiveté about black cultural and social issues. Most have encountered strained relationships across the color line. All are dedicated to promoting strong self-accepting children. They readily acknowledge that people whom they encounter are "always trying to figure out the mystery of biracial children."

Fostering Identities of Color

Almost all these white mothers expected that their children would have an African American or biracial identity. They perceive their husbands as being crucial to their children's racial identity development and understanding of racial realities in American society. As one mother said, while she and her husband share similar parenting views with regard to race, "He really knows what the reality is and I don't." Nevertheless, these white mothers independently or with their spouses have implemented strategies to develop and reinforce positive identities of color in their children. Some have consciously chosen to live in racially and economically diverse neighborhoods where their children can interact with others who look like them. Some have chosen to send their children to Afrocentric schools and many have chosen to send their children to racially diverse summer camps. Many mothers emphasize the importance of international travel and exposure to other cultures. All have friendship circles that include other biracial families.

Encountering Strained Relationships Across the Color Line

White mothers spoke of strained relationships across the color line within their families and among their acquaintances. Many had experienced disapproval and opposition to their interracial marriages from their own families and occasionally from their husbands' families. While for some familial opposition attenuated over time, for others it has persisted unabated. One woman's mother has never visited her daughter's home, though her grandchild visits her white grandmother, who lives in another city. Another woman recalled that her daughter daily telephoned her faraway black grandmother but rarely her equally distant white grandmother. Another woman mentioned that her husband's family continued to have difficulty with her being white and her lack of religious affiliation, though she and her husband have been together for many years. Yet another woman noted with regret that while her son is close to his white relatives, he has no relationship with his black father or with his father's family. Another woman recalled how her husband's cousin had excluded her from an invitation to an African American club that was extended to her husband and their children. In fact, several mentioned that they did not always feel accepted in black social settings and that their friendship circles were predominantly biracial or white.

These white women's stories illustrate the reality of prejudice against interracial families from both sides of the color line today. Many experience strained relationships across the color line in their extended families and among their acquaintances. These women, however, perceive that today there is greater acceptance of interracial partners and biracial children than in the era of their youth and anticipate that the generation of their grandchildren will encounter fewer strained relationships and less tension about the experience of being black.

Coping with Cultural Naiveté

White mothers who are perceptive about racial realities acknowledge that they do not have the experiential knowledge of race in America that their black husbands have. They are culturally naïve—in varying degrees—about being black in the United States. Recognition of their naiveté leads many white mothers to defer to their spouses for interpretations of racial matters and for strategic responses to racial incidents.

Almost all white mothers admit that they have issues about how to care for their children's curly hair. They do not know how to cope with tight curls—how to comb and brush them, how to braid them, or how to straighten them. One mother recounted how an African American teacher in her daughter's school recommended a beauty salon where she could take her daughter and how an

African American woman stopped her on the street to advise what kind of hair preparation to use on her daughter's unruly hair. An African American mother said that white mothers of biracial children had stopped her numerous times in drug stores for advice on hair care. White mothers, then, rarely know how to cope effectively with caring for curly hair.

White mothers cope not only with their own cultural naiveté about racial matters but the perceptual naiveté of others. Strangers may assume that a mother and her child are not related, because they differ in appearance or they may assume that a child is adopted, or Hispanic, or simply not related to its mother. Asserting their maternal relationship is as necessary for white mothers of biracial children as for black mothers of biracial children.

Promoting Self-Acceptance

When white mothers reflect on the challenges and rewards of parenting biracial children, they emphasize the importance of promoting their children's self-acceptance. They stress the importance of talking openly about issues of concern, about knowing and understanding both parents' cultures, about encouraging their children to accept people as individuals rather than prejudging them, and about exposing their children to cultural differences. White mothers also discuss some of the challenges that they face in rearing their children. Some mothers have confronted teachers' low academic expectations of their children. Most children have encountered racist slurs or social rejection by other children at some time in their young lives. In such instances, the mothers with whom we talked directly confronted the situations with parents and teachers of the rejecting children. Challenging stereotypes and racist behavior is important for these white mothers in seeking to ensure that their children will develop strong senses of self and racial identity.

Summing Up

Racially aware white mothers with young children at home confront many of the same challenges as their black counterparts and also some distinctive ones. They, too, have the challenge of fostering positive biracial identities and confronting strained relations across the color line. They have the additional challenge of coping with their own cultural naiveté about race in the United States. Having grown up as privileged white people in the United States, they have learned about and experienced aspects of racial realities as adults. Since they acknowledge their experiential naiveté about racial matters, they tend to defer to their spouses in interpreting and strategically responding to racial issues as they parent their biracial children.

RACE-AVOIDING MOTHERS

While most of the women with whom we talked consider that nurturing racial identity and promoting self-acceptance in their biracial children are critical aspects of their mothering, several women avoid reference to race in preparing their children for adulthood. They are loving parents who care deeply about their children's development, but as mothers they do not focus on racial matters. Some of these woman are African American, often light-skinned, and some are European Americans. All are engaged in professional work in universities, research organizations, commercial enterprises, or home offices. Some are rearing young and adolescent children at home; others have older children who are away in college or in the world of work. While they may be aware of racial issues, as mothers they are reactive rather than proactive with respect to race in the lives of their children.

Avoiding Racial Identities

At birth, these mothers did not have notions of possible racial identities of their children, and they have continued to do little to nurture their children's identities as people of color. Several averred that they had no expectations about their children's racial identities at birth; rather, they focused on pregnancy and impending motherhood. One African American woman, however, stated that she expected her child to be African American and another that she supposed her child would be biracial. Not only did these mothers not have well-defined conceptions of possible racial identities for their children at birth but they have also continued to ignore race in parenting their children. As one mother said: "I don't want [my child's] life to be based on race or based on that identification. I'd like it to be based on the fact that she's a good individual, she's a good contributor to society, that she understands society, that she's well read."

Avoidance of racial identity on the part of these mothers appears to be mirrored in their children's self-identities. Several mothers stated that their young children did not think of themselves in racial terms. One mother thought that her adult children considered themselves biracial but was not certain that they did, while another believed that her children considered themselves African American. When one young African American mother told her blond son that he was black, he responded, "Yeah, Mom, I know I'm black, but I'm not really black."

Their children's appearance and their spouses' (black and white) indifference to racial identity have facilitated these mothers' avoidance of racial identity issues. To the casual observer many of their children appear to be white, especially if they are alone with their European American fathers. Moreover, these women's white husbands defer to them on racial matters or their black husbands do not emphasize race in their family discourse. The politics of race are rarely discussed in their homes; their friendship circles are not intentionally racially diverse; their children choose not to participate in multiracial organizations in school or college. Moreover, in some cases these mothers' upper-middle-class status may have shielded them from the most insidious racial challenges. Thus, light skin privilege and economic privilege have enabled these mothers to avoid confronting racial identity issues.

Meeting Racial Challenges

However much these mothers seek to avoid racial identifications and to insulate their families from racial conundrums, they nevertheless have encountered racial challenges from family members, strangers, and their children. One mother's parents strongly opposed her marriage to an African American, though her family has come to embrace their biracial grandchildren. Without exception these mothers have encountered challenges to their relationships with their children from strangers. In supermarkets people have stared curiously at them when accompanied by their children. Casual business acquaintances and teachers have asked if their children are adopted; strangers have inquired whether or not they are their children's nannies. They have answered by asserting their maternal ties to children who look different from them—who are lighter or darker than they. Inevitably, many of their children have come home with tales of racial incidents, which their mothers must confront. Rather than anticipating and preparing strategically for such confrontations, a black mother said, "We talk about things as they come up." In the opinion of a white mother: "When you're raising kids, you're raising kids day by day. As opportunities present themselves, you sit down with them."

Confessing to Racial Awareness

Although these mothers seek to avoid racial categories and to insulate themselves and their children from race matters, they variously acknowledge the role of racial considerations in their parenting. Most emphasize the importance of their children knowing both their African American and their European American families. One mother regretted that many of her African American relatives have died so that her younger child does not have the opportunity to know them as her older child did. Another African American mother was pleased that her child knew both sides of his family but confessed that she "was not a provider of racially specific and positive materials over the years," as her mother had been for her. Yet another, who eschews racial descriptors, acknowledged that she feared her child might someday experience racial rejection. One mother who consistently avoided race matters in parenting confessed that she and her husband had chosen a multiracial neighborhood in which to raise their children. Despite protestations of race avoidance, these mothers are likely to face—at some stage—the potential role of race in their biracial children's lives.

Accounting for Race Avoidance

Mothers of young biracial children acknowledge that parenting biracial children today is different from a generation ago. They perceive that there is less concern with racial labeling and greater acceptance of people of color than in the past. Moreover, most of their children are racially ambiguous in their appearance. Some appear to be European American to strangers; others are thought to be Asian or Latin American. Their appearances shield them from some racial inequities. Their mothers hope that the world is changing and becoming more accepting of children like them. They reinforce that hope by avoiding race matters as much as possible in their parenting.

Summing Up

Several women with whom we talked preferred to respond reactively rather than proactively to racial issues in rearing their biracial children. Neither they nor their children stress racial identity. Insulated by their socioeconomic status from some racial concerns, these mothers are nevertheless aware of the potential importance of race matters in the lives of their children.

COMMON PARENTING THEMES AMONG MOTHERS OF BIRACIAL CHILDREN

Irrespective of whether or not a woman considers that cultivating racial awareness is significant in parenting her biracial children, her children are racially ambiguous in the world outside the home where her relationship to them is likely to be challenged at one time or another. Most mothers, but not all, with whom we talked believe that it is important to prepare their children proactively for the vicissitudes that they may encounter around race as they mature. These women stress the importance of providing children with multicultural experiences and relationships. Although many mentioned the importance of living in a multicultural and multiracial neighborhood where families like theirs and people of color are more common, few do. Almost without exception, the mothers with whom we talked perceive that American society is becoming more racially diverse and that future biracial generations will find social acceptance more readily than earlier ones.

White women, whether mothers of young or adult children, discussed the opposition of their natal families to their interracial marriages more often than black women. Usually, but not always, white families eventually accepted the biracial family. Yet both black women with Jewish spouses and white Jewish women more frequently experienced protracted and unrelenting familial rejection than other women. Moreover, both black and white women of older children mentioned strained social relationships from both sides of the color line.

Mothers of older children recalled that as young parents there was a dearth of information about biraciality available to new parents and fewer institutional supports for families like theirs than there are today. Citing the increased number of interracial marriages and biracial children, the women with whom we talked are optimistic about the social acceptance of children like theirs in the twenty-first-century United States.

NOTES

1. See Appendix I.

2. Source: U.S. Census Bureau, Current Population Survey, 2006 Annual Social and Economic Supplement.

3. In 2006, 19.5 percent of married Asian women and 7.2 percent of married Asian men had a non-Asian spouse.

4. Joel Williamson, *New People: Miscegnation and Mulattoes in the United States* (New York: The Free Press, 1980), 188–89; Paul R. Spickard, *Mixed Blood: Intermarriage and Ethnic Identity in Twentieth Century America* (Madison: University of Wisconsin Press, 1989), 281, 308.

5. See Table 1 and Appendix II.

6. Peggy McIntosh pioneered the exploration of "white privilege" in her pathbreaking essay, "White Privilege and Male Privilege: A Personal Account of Coming To See Correspondences through Work in Women Studies," Working Paper 189, Wellesley College for Research on Women, 1988.

7. Haya El Basser, "Fewer call themselves multiracial," *USA TODAY*, May 4–6, 2007, 7.

3

Profiles of Mothers of Biracial Children

I am the person I am because of my marriage and my motherhood, and that's related to the fact that I am the mother of biracial children.

In this chapter we are presenting profiles of some of the mothers with whom we talked about their experiences rearing biracial children. We have clustered the profiles into three groups: African American mothers, biracial mothers who self-identify as African Americans, and European American mothers. The differing perspectives of the mothers within each group and the commonalities of views across clusters suggest the rich variety of parenting philosophies and experiences of mothers of biracial children across and within generations and races.

AFRICAN AMERICAN MOTHERS

Profile 1: Carol, Mother of an Adult Son and a Daughter

The African American mother of a son, Thomas, and a daughter, Martha, both in their thirties, Carol recalled her son as a first-grader reported that someone had asked what his race was. She said he seemed to understand that he was half black and half white, but he wanted to know which half. After questioning him, she realized that "which half" meant he wanted to know whether a vertical or a horizontal line separated the halves. When she replied, "Neither," she said that ended the discussion. "It didn't seem traumatic; it just seemed curious. That's all." In retrospect, she wishes she had "found out more" about what race and being biracial meant to her children. She added that now there is literature for and about multiracial and biracial children, which did not exist when her children were young. She remarked: "It's probably not accidental that my daughter's best friend from first grade was another biracial child." Recently married, her son's wife is biracial and her daughter's boyfriend is biracial.

Carol and her husband, Seth, have lived in the Boston area since they were married in 1969. He is an attorney; she is on the faculty of a university. Reared as an orthodox Jew, Seth is used to being in an "out-group," according to Carol. He understands that race is a "bigger deal than being Jewish in this country, and much more negative stuff comes with it."

One example of "negative stuff" occurred when Thomas was in nursery school. A white mother had a neighborhood birthday party for her child and "everybody was invited except Thomas," Carol related. A name-calling incident on the part of a neighbor's child was followed by an apology from the child's mother. At a later age, hyper-surveillance in stores, specifically in FAO Schwartz, was among her negative recollections.

Negative experiences were offset by her children's experience at the Advent School, a private elementary school in Boston. Multicultural and socioeconomically diverse, the school's curriculum and programs fostered the healthy development of racial identity. Both Thomas and Martha completed secondary school at Boston Latin School, the premier Boston public secondary school.

Racial identity, skin color, and religion figured in Carol's account. She mentioned that members of her family come in a wide range of hues. Although her children regard themselves as African Americans, Carol stated that their self-perceptions may be more complicated. Martha, described as light-skinned, in an Indian restaurant was taken for Indian. Thomas, who is a little darker than Martha, has been mistaken as Dominican.

Christmas holidays were spent with Carol's brother's family. Her children enjoyed contacts with their cousins, Carol's nephews, slightly older than her own children. She mentioned that they "did not have much to do with" her husband's family in upstate New York. Seth's family had objected to the marriage. Her parents went to visit Seth's parents in Schenectady, but were turned away. She recalled two visits at the home of her in-laws when their children were young. The children did not view Seth's parents as relatives. She added: "I don't know whether or not we explained who they were." At Passover the family always had at least one Seder with friends in Newton, a Boston suburb.

Carol said she had definite ideas about childrearing. It is important, she asserted, for them to be around people of different races. Her close and lifelong relationship with a Japanese American family was an expression of that sentiment. She feels that she still has time to talk with her children about how being biracial is different from being monoracial. Her husband, she said, probably felt that she was an overprotective parent. Her defense: "I've tried to tell him that I came from overprotective parents and, furthermore, that it was necessary to be overprotective." She feels her attitude toward childrearing was "racially formed," that you cannot leave things to chance.

Carol is pleased with the upbringing of Thomas and Martha and proud of their accomplishments. Thomas, who has a law degree, is a journalist; Martha is a doctoral candidate in neuroscience. She mentioned their involvement in race-related matters as college students. At this stage, she wonders if they will have to deal with being educational elites, not that she knows how that will influence their identity. She hopes that they will regard as significant the multicultural contacts and settings that she fashioned for them in their formative years.

With hindsight, Carol regrets her failing to probe what race had meant to her children while they were growing up. In the absence of literature, organizations, and public discourse on biracial experience, she lacked resources and missed opportunities to explore the impact of the "negative stuff" they encountered. The racial identity of her children appears more salient than their association with their paternal Jewish lineage. She values their multicultural exposure as a contribution to their identity formation and considers the relevance of their being "educational elites."

Profile 2: Leslie and Her Daughter

Leslie, a fifty-two-year-old African American woman, directs a Boston cultural institution and is married to a white now-retired Protestant minister who served black congregations for most of his career. Their daughter, Samantha, was born eight years after her parents married, because, Leslie said, "The notion of having children did not exactly appeal to me given the state of the world." Before Samantha was born, Leslie helped to raise two of her husband's four children by a previous marriage. Laughingly Leslie said, "The name of my book is going to be *How I, A Black Woman, Raised My White Stepdaughter To Be Puerto Rican*," because two of her stepdaughters have married Puerto Ricans. Leslie is close to her own extended black family and her husband's white children, their spouses, and grandchildren. Her professional and friendship networks are equally diverse.

When Samantha was born, Leslie anticipated that her racial identity would be African American: "Defining the child as African American has much to do with my pride in what that tradition and legacy is and with girding her against the reality of the world—that there is no escaping being African American." Leslie talks with pride of her family heritage with its origin in a great-great-grandfather who owned property in Georgia, still held in trust by his descendants. Samantha at twelve, however, self-identifies as black-and-white and is very aware that her identity is shaped by the fact that she has a black mother and a white father. She has criticized her mother for having more pictures of African Americans than of white people on the walls of their home.

When Samantha was five years old, the family moved from their home in urban Connecticut to a suburban town near Boston, Massachusetts. Samantha did not want to make the move, but when she arrived in her new home, her mother reports that she said, "'Okay, you did this to me. The least you could do is get me a biracial babysitter.' And we said, 'What do you mean? You want a babysitter who's like you?' She just kept saying 'Someone who's just like me—they have a black mother and a white father.'" Leslie's husband met a biracial high school girl who was willing to become Samantha's babysitter. After Samantha met and talked with the girl, she complained to her parents, "She's not like me. Her mother's white and her dad's black. It's an entirely different thing."

Recently in Sunday school Samantha has had to assert her biraciality with a friend who insisted that he was white and she was black. She tried but failed to convince him that "Yes, you're white, but I'm white and black." Assertion and counter-assertion continued until at last Samantha said, "Okay, fine. You're just throwing this out. You don't want to know who I am. I asked you what you were."

In school Samantha also has had a number of negative experiences around race that she and her parents have addressed tactfully but forcefully. In first grade, for example, she had difficulty with another girl who tried to bully her by preventing her from using her locker and saying racially disparaging things to her. The day after Samantha confessed this experience to her mother, Leslie and her husband went to the school and they insisted on speaking to the teacher. The teacher agreed to address the issue in a way that would not identify Samantha as the victim to the other children. Looking back, Leslie is proud of how she and her husband handled this incident. Leslie recalls that she and her husband said to Samantha, "When there is an injustice you deal with it immediately. And you deal with it kindly and you ask good people to help you."

Leslie noted that Samantha has become aware that she is treated differently when she is with her father and when she is with her mother. A recent incident concerned trying to buy an expensive pen. The salesperson implied that Leslie would be unable to afford such a pen, which the store did not stock because of its costliness.

In reflecting on key considerations in raising biracial children, Leslie said, "I think one is that you've got to believe that the world is good enough to receive them and that they will make it the beloved community that [Martin Luther] King talked about. You've got to believe that. Otherwise, you ought not to do it, because how they see the world is very different than how you do." She also considers that "providing images and people who are like them" is important in nurturing biracial children. She concluded: "I think that this wonderful adventure [of parenting biracial children] that we deliberately engaged in ought to make us better people and whether or not we actually achieve that is another thing, but I think it has all the potential of making us better parents, better human beings, if we open our hearts to it."

Explicit in her commitment to interracial life and social justice, Leslie embarked on motherhood with a high level of racial awareness. With the involvement of both black and white kinship networks and their association with colleagues, friends, and neighbors, Leslie and her husband have created a supportive, racially diverse climate for their daughter. They recognize the challenges for families with biracial children and use racial incidents as teaching opportunities to demonstrate how to confront such situations with force and tact. Leslie's expression of pride and satisfaction with their parenting experience is noteworthy. She appreciates the potential for personal growth and deepening relationships as parents of biracial offspring.

Profile 3: Denise and Her Daughters

Denise, a dark-skinned African American homemaker in her late forties, is the mother of three biracial daughters who range in age from twenty to thirteen and in color from very light to dark. She grew up in a predominantly white Boston suburb, and trained and worked as a mathematician before devoting herself full-time to childrearing. During her marriage to Mark, a red-haired computer scientist, Denise has followed his career from Maryland through Colorado to California and back to Massachusetts. For the past eight years Denise and her family have lived in a predominantly white Boston suburb, fairly close to her childhood town.

Color differences within the family have led to uncomfortable neighborhood and school experiences. Denise has had to assert her children's African American racial identity in schools in California and Massachusetts. Denise said that in California her eldest daughter sometimes was identified as Mexican, while the children's school principal assumed that she was the mother of three dark-skinned African American children rather than her own. Denise remarked: "I saw him all the time. We lived there for three years and . . . yet he had no idea who my children were." In her Massachusetts town she encountered a similar problem with her youngest daughter's kindergarten teacher, who could not tell which of the two black children in her class of seventeen kindergartners was Denise's child. Denise concluded her description of the situation by saying, "I found the experience very irritating and really very distressing." Moreover, her older children were identified as white in their school records until Denise insisted on having them changed.

The negative experiences of Denise's children around issues of race and color in school probably have contributed to their ambivalence about their racial identity. Although Denise anticipated that her children would self-identify as black, she has not addressed racial identity explicitly with them: "I realize that I probably should have talked with them more about race than I did, because they've ended up confused [about their racial identities]." Her youngest and darkest daughter as a preschooler did not identify herself as black: "She said, 'I don't like my black swimming teacher, because black people don't speak English.' . . . That was surprising to me—that she really did not self-identify with being black and that she had the same kind of global outlook on blacks and whites just from lack of exposure."

In a sense, Denise's silence around racial issues with her children mirrors her own experience growing up: "My mother is a light-skinned black and her hair was light brown, so my mother always called it 'good hair'—it used to drive me crazy. She was as fair as my eldest daughter, so she had to choose whether [or not] to identify as black; my dad is quite dark-skinned." Her mother's grandmother, however, declared that Denise's mother was "'far too dark.' And my mother remembers the fireworks that took place after that—her mother kicking her mother-in-law out. But that had to have influenced my mother's feelings about race. And as a result, we didn't talk about race at all. We talked about lots of things, but we really didn't talk about race."

Nevertheless, in considering important factors in rearing biracial children, Denise thinks that parents should talk to children about race, though she acknowledges that she is "not very good at it. But I do bring things up." She considers children should feel comfortable responding to "stereotypes associated with skin color and that's the part that I try to talk to them about—just a little bit different from cultural heritage."

Another important consideration for Denise is the neighborhood in which she chooses to live. She looks for neighborhoods that "are a little more open-minded. I try to live close to a university and I'm learning if there's a lot of art, it's a little more cosmopolitan." She, however, does not think that the neighborhood in which she currently lives provides that kind of open acceptance. Just as her parents raised her in white neighborhoods, she feels, "I've done the same thing with my children—an Irish neighborhood in an upper-class town. I have no concept of my neighbors' experience, because I didn't go to school with them."

Denise acknowledges her feelings of isolation and wishes that she had more support from other families like hers. She, however, has found that in her town people of color "try to assimilate too much," and that consequently whites work more on diversity issues than people of color. She concluded, "I just found that really bizarre."

Denise brings to motherhood some unresolved issues related to racial appearance derived from her own upbringing. She understands the importance of discussing racial matters with children and regrets her inability to engage her daughters more deeply in conversations about race. She finds them confused and ambivalent about racial identity. She also has regrets and reservations about school and neighborhood choices that she and her husband have made. She herself feels isolated in their suburban enclave. She reflects on having grown up in white neighborhoods and now bringing up her children in white neighborhoods where they experience social distance. There is little evidence of the contributions of her family or her husband's family in shaping the racial identities of their daughters, nor do family friendships seem central to their childrearing.

Profile 4: Sherry and Her Daughter

The African American mother of a five-year-old daughter named Thalia, Sherry recalled her initial formulation of Thalia's racial identity:

> Okay, I'm black, she's black—but, of course, she's mixed. My husband and I actually talked about this in depth for years after she was born, because schools around town actually asked the question. . . . We were happy that the birth certificate didn't ask what the race was. We had to obviously confront it and do something, writing something . . . on the applications of the three schools we ap-

plied to. We said . . . "Thalia's mother is black; Thalia's father is white. She is a blend of the two of us."

She described Thalia's hair and eyes: "She's got a bit of my curl in her hair; she has her Daddy's really thin hair . . . eyes like my grandfather on my mother's side." She said they prefer to talk about physical characteristics in terms of genetics rather than race.

Sherry said that Thalia has expressed awareness of differences as follows: "Mommy, your skin is brown, my skin is cream, Daddy's is white." Sherry has observed that recently Thalia has talked about brown skin, more from color identification than racial identification.

> We've talked about texture of hair and the different hues. One of her cousins is in her opinion a dark chocolate. [Another] cousin who is her father's niece is cream, in her opinion, with yellow hair. Although she knows blond, she talks about it in terms of color instead of race. When the topic comes up we will talk about it. We are getting a few books on the subject. When you live with a professor, you get a book on the subject.

Sherry, a banking lawyer, and her historian husband met thirty years ago in their Washington, D.C., high school. They live in an upper-middle-class Cambridge, Massachusetts, neighborhood where Thalia attends a private school. When Thalia was younger—in a stroller—a woman in their neighborhood mistook Sherry to be

Thalia's nanny: "My chin went up a couple of notches. I said, 'I'm her mother. Her nanny is not with us.'" Sherry stated that was the only race-related incident they have encountered. She feels insulated by living in a neighborhood that "is a little bit different from any other place."

They frequently visit their extended family in Washington where Thalia sees her relatives—black and white. Sherry's family is "quick to ensure she has black dolls" and books illustrated with brown children. She added: "We have all sorts of music you would identify with the black race in this house . . . my family ensures it."

Sherry anticipates more questions from Thalia as she grows older and situations that will require parental attention:

> We expect many more questions about differences. We try to talk about how everyone is different as opposed to you're different, because your mother's black and your father's white. Her cousin is different because of how she looks and she looks different from her mother. We try to talk about those sorts of things, because we do think that self-identification is important first. . . . We're expecting to have to talk more about it. As I say, we're preparing by looking at reference books.

She added, "My husband doesn't think it's going to be a big topic. He thinks that the society is beyond that . . . but I'm waiting for it. . . . He sees children evolving into a different world. I still come from the black perspective—

growing up in the 1960s, having a father very much involved in civil rights and still believing somebody is out there to hurt my child. I'm watching for it."

Sherry referred to a book she has found useful—*Raising a Mixed Child in White America*. It has drawn her attention to their environment and the children Thalia plays with. She has a "nice selection of children she plays with—it's a rainbow." An important consideration in her view of childrearing is to ensure that "they have their own identity before they have a racial identity. . . . The key is establishing confidence and self-confidence."

Sherry and her husband have an intellectualized approach to childrearing, relying on books for guidance with regard to their young daughter's racial acculturation. Explicit in their discussions of skin color, Thalia may understand that she is a blend. Their visits to relatives—white and black—who take an interest in Thalia probably reinforce her biracial identity, although she may not yet comprehend race as a concept. Despite her husband's opinion that race will be of little importance in the future, Sherry is wary and vigilant, preparing to counter offensive race-related situations.

Profile 5: Jane and Her Two Sons

Jane's two sons are in their mid- to late-twenties; she is approaching sixty. Jane grew up in the Midwest with a large extended African American family, which included some interracial marriages in an older generation and some relatives who have claimed a white racial identity. She has been married for more than thirty years to a prominent white academic doctor. Originally trained as a nurse, Jane is now an educational consultant but when her children were adolescents, she owned a children's multicultural bookstore.

Early in their marriage Jane and her husband worked for several years as clinicians in Tanzania, where their older son was born. When they returned to the United States, they settled in a multiracial Cambridge neighborhood. Jane's family has lived in the same house on a quiet tree-shaded street in Cambridge since their return from Africa. Its décor reflected their cosmopolitan interest in African and African American culture. Although the family has traveled widely in the United States and abroad, they feel most comfortable in a racially and economically heterogeneous Cambridge neighborhood.

When her sons were born, Jane anticipated that they would identify themselves as "black," though she said that she did not think much about their racial identity until they were in their teens. Her sons today consider themselves to be "biracial." Both, however, found clarifying their racial identity challenging during their adolescent years. In college her older son joined the Biracial Students Club. At the time he told her, "This is something that you and Dad will never know, because you are not biracial. This is something that the black person cannot know about and the white person cannot know about."

Although as a younger parent Jane emphasized her African American heritage with her children, she later appreciated that her children should also be aware of her husband's distinctive family background. "Even though white culture is there all the time," she recognized that "it may not have been [my husband's]." Jane researched both her husband's and her own family histories to create a book for her children about their family backgrounds. As a family they have attended annual family reunions of black and white relatives in the Midwest. Jane and her husband have "encouraged them to embrace both sides" of their heritage.

Jane considers that she and her husband have played complementary parenting roles: she as lenient nurturer, he as nurturing disciplinarian: "And as the kids got older, they looked to us for different things—they would look to me for more nurturing but when they had a big decision, they would go to him." Turning to contexts outside their family lives, Jane said:

> And then as my kids got to school age, I joined Jack and Jill, because I wanted to meet other middle-class black families.[1] We did that until they graduated from high school. I was more interested for them, but I needed some black women in my life as well. I think it was hard for my husband. He's always been very supportive, when you think about joining Jack and Jill and going to my family reunion every year and having a lot of black friends.

Jane made an effort to bring into racial balance the influence of her African American heritage and her husband's family history in rearing their two sons, who regard
themselves as biracial. Brought up in a racially and socioeconomically diverse Cambridge neighborhood, her sons
enjoy supportive contacts with both the maternal and paternal extended families. Still, Jane sought the company of
black women through an organization that also afforded
contacts for her sons with other middle-class black children. Jane expresses a sense of satisfaction with her sons'
coming to terms with being biracial and their knowing
that it is different from being merely black or white.

Profile 6: Harriet and Her Son

Married forty years to Mitchell, a physicist she described as "culturally Jewish," Harriet recalled the remark
of an aunt on her side of the family who announced that
their newborn son, Isaac (now thirty-five), looked like a
"little Jewish baby." She wryly stated that she had expected
him to be identified as black and that he grew a shade
darker as he grew older. In his early years, Isaac attended a
"relatively integrated" daycare center at the university
where Harriet was dean of students. In his elementary
school there were very few black children; in their neighborhood, Isaac's closest friendship was with a Japanese
American boy.

As a young adult, Isaac reported significant race-
related incidents that had occurred in his pre-teen years
when other boys called him "names," intimidated him, and

picked fights. At the time he felt that he himself needed to handle such situations, that his sense of self-worth was related to his ability to deal with his peers. Learning about this phase of his experience stirred feelings of inadequacy in Harriet, who asked, "Where was I? What was I thinking? Why wasn't I aware?" In retrospect, she regretted having missed opportunities for "conversations" that would have made some connections between the liberal-to-radical opinions expressed in their household and the realities of the social environment Isaac had encountered in their neighborhood and at school. During his childhood and adolescence, Isaac recalled feeling isolated and being seen as a loner. Harriet regards his sense of isolation as detrimental to his self-esteem. Despite recognition of his intellectual potential, for several years Isaac was an underachiever. Only in recent years have his self-expectations heightened. Harriet views her failure to recognize and address his early isolation as a shortcoming.

Visits with Harriet's relatives in Cleveland, Ohio, exposure to cultural experiences that heightened awareness of African American contributions, and attendance with Harriet at civil rights demonstrations were intentional means of reinforcing Isaac's racial identity.

Harriet's in-laws have had infrequent and distant contact with Isaac. She said that Mitchell's mother, whom Harriet never met, was very upset by their marriage. (His father had died prior to their marriage.) At age sixteen, Isaac finally met his paternal grandmother, who died soon thereafter. Mitchell has a brother and a sister. His sister maintains a "cordial distance," while his brother, who lives in California, was persuaded to cultivate a relationship with them. In an exchange of visits, Isaac has come to know his uncle and cousins.

Harriet offered the following advice: foremost among considerations in rearing biracial children are the value of contact with other biracial children and opportunities to discuss their experiences. Formal contacts among parents of biracial children would be beneficial. Parents need to be aware of influences and contacts children have outside the home and potential consequences of situations that occur. Opportunities for children to share their experiences with parents in a spirit of support and affirmation are also useful.

In retrospect, Harriet was candid, thoughtful, and regretful about opportunities missed for conversations about racial and social realities her son encountered in childhood and adolescence. As an adult, Isaac related incidents in his silent struggle with racism that contributed to the social isolation he had known. Growing up culturally Jewish, but with little contact with Jewish relatives, he was better acquainted with Harriet's family and African American cultural contributions. She finds him in his mid-thirties still uncertain about whether he is black or biracial, and she feels there is tension on his part about his Jewish background. Harriet's reflections on their situation elicited useful suggestions for nurturing biracial children.

AFRICAN AMERICAN–IDENTIFIED BIRACIAL MOTHERS
Profile 7: Sarah and Her Young Daughters

Sarah, a Harvard-trained corporate real estate lawyer in her late thirties, has been married to Tom, a technical college-trained Scottish plumber, for thirteen years. Sarah is biracial—her mother is white, her father is black—but she identifies herself as African American. At the time of our conversation with her, her daughters were four years old and one year old.

She and her husband hope that their children will embrace both their racial and ethnic heritages: "So the racial identity that I'd like them to grow into is that I'd like them to see themselves as both Scottish and African American. To have them see themselves from a racial standpoint as a person of color and yet as a white person, because they have that duality with their parents." Nevertheless, Sarah acknowledges that they may not grow into that reality, "because I do think your phenotype and what you appear to look like and external influences that you experience because of how you look impact your sense of how you come to your own identity." Since her children are very fair, she acknowledges that when they are not with her, strangers are likely to perceive them as white.

Sarah was very articulate about the intentional way in which she and her husband have selected the neighborhood in which they live, chosen the activities in which their children participate, and discuss racial and ethnic identities in their home. They have chosen to live in a multiracial and multicultural neighborhood of Boston where they as a couple and they and their children as a family are perceived as "normal" and not "odd," as her biracial family-of-origin was perceived in its suburban neighborhood. "On our street we have a multiracial lesbian couple, we have biracial heterosexual couples, we have Latino families, we have Irish Catholic families. It's just a nice mix and that's true around our larger neighborhood in terms of cookouts and things." The diversity of their neighborhood is mirrored in their friendship patterns.

In their family, Sarah is the self-professed organizer of extracurricular activities. She chose to send their elder daughter to swimming classes at the Roxbury YMCA because its attendees were predominantly African American, rather than to classes at the West Roxbury YMCA, which was predominantly white. Similarly, she chose dance classes emphasizing African dance rather than a more conventional European dance school. While her older daughter is the lightest child in both settings, her daughter is comfortable in both.

Sarah and her husband speak of people's racial and cultural identities when they talk with their children. They want their children to realize "that it's a descriptive thing to recognize someone's race; it's not offensive, and when you don't do that, you don't recognize an element of them."

Sarah, like the other mothers with whom we talked, has encountered people who challenged her relationship with her children. In her experience white people are often unable to see the relationship that people of color usually recognize immediately.

Sarah thinks that race is more fluid in her children's generation of biracial Americans than it was for hers:

> I remember my mom once saying, "When you guys were born, I was glad that it was clear that you were African American." She had a sense that we would be seen as belonging to a particular racial group as opposed to people saying "What are you?" . . . In a world that was so black and white, being able to put your foot firmly in one or the other might make your navigation through that kind of racialized society easier. . . . I know people who are biracial who can't easily be identified as black or white struggle much more, and I think that will be true for my kids. . . . So long as I'm not around, most people will think they're Caucasian. I think they will struggle a lot with that. But I think that in American society it's "in" to be mixed now in a way that it wasn't "in" in the sixties. It's a very hip thing. I'm always astounded—look at the advertisements.

As a parent of biracial children, Sarah perceives that an important difference between her and her own children's experience is that she is the parent of color, whereas her own mother is white.

> The truth is my mom doesn't know what it's like to be black or to be biracial for that matter. That's going to

change the dynamic [between me and my children]. . . . So there are those insights that my mom just never had that I have and will help me to be able to have conversations with my children that maybe I didn't even recognize that I knew I needed when I was younger, but also I think that I'll understand some of the conflicts more. And I think that's the most profound difference between me as the parent of biracial children and my mom as the mother of biracial children.

An assertive, affirmative individual, Sarah draws on her own biracial childhood experience as a psychological and ideological advantage with regard to mothering biracial children. She fosters in her daughters an African American identification despite their physical appearance. At the same time, their paternal Scottish heritage is also cultivated, adding an international dimension to their identity discourse. Their deliberate choice of a multiracial neighborhood and racially and ethnically diverse activities support biracial identity. Still, Sarah anticipates her daughters' fair skin may create future identity issues.

Profile 8: Marie and Her Son

Interviewed in a conference room at the Boston law school where she teaches, biracial Marie, who identifies herself as African American, assumed her son would be biracial when he was born nine years ago. After all, "three of his four grandparents are white." Her African American father died when James was three years old. She said James knew her father, but she did not expand on their relationship. Given his appearance, she is not surprised that James does not think of himself as belonging to "any one group."

Enrolled in a predominately white private school in Cambridge, Massachusetts, James has declined invitations to the school's "children of color lunch." Marie reported with embarrassed amusement that he has always told his teachers that he didn't want to attend. She said that she will not insist that he join them at lunch. She said James, a history buff, has a "fair sense" of racial awareness. Recalling a scene when she read him a story about Abraham Lincoln, James asked what Lincoln did to help the slaves. In her response, she told him what Lincoln did and added that emancipation was not enough. "He watches the news on television, so he knows that things happen to people because of their race."

With respect to individuals who have shaped James's racial awareness, Marie mentioned a woman from the Ivory Coast who was their nanny when they lived in Washington, D.C. She characterized her mother, James's occasional caretaker, as someone who has a "difficult time with race because, when she married my father in the fifties," her family opposed the marriage. While her mother is highly aware of the relevance of race, Marie doubts that she would initiate a discussion about racial matters with her grandson. Bob, James's father, was said to talk about race in the context of sports, informing James of the importance of the Negro baseball league and prominence of black players in other sports. Their friendship and professional networks occasionally expose James to African Americans.

She worries about the day when James will be rejected, hurt, or offended because of racial bias, fears he won't be as prepared "as some other kids" for the experience of rejection. Uncertain about how to prepare him, she said, "I don't want him to be like my mother, who sees rejection and evil when it's not there." She added, "I'm sure my parents were always worried about [me]—what are people going to do . . . going to say . . . what's their reaction going to be?"

As for Bob's view, she thinks he wants James to grow up with "a sense of who he is in all respects . . . he does not worry that he'll not recognize that people will perceive him—label him—as an African American kid."

Marie, who is biracial, understands her son—given that he has three white grandparents—has the physical appearance of a white boy. She infers that he does not identify with people of color; she herself has not formulated a position on James' racial orientation. They live in a predominantly white suburb, and her son attends a private school where white pupils and faculty are the overwhelming majority. If he is not viewed as biracial does not seem to be a significant issue in their situation. Although Marie's maternity was challenged when James was an infant, she seems reluctant to imbue him with a sense of racial awareness. Her reference to her white mother's racial sensitivity may have blunted her concerns about race. Because she thinks James may look more African American as he grows older, Marie anticipates a time when he may be hurt or offended by racial bias. She expects he will not be equipped for such encounters, and she remains uncertain about the means of preparation.

Profile 9: Catherine and Her Daughters

In her mid-forties, Catherine has been married for twenty-five years but has been a parent for only nine. Her reluctance to become a mother, she said, was related to working out issues with her adoptive mother. Catherine's adoptive parents were older African Americans; her birth mother was white. For most of her life, Catherine has considered her racial identity to be "African American," though she is "learning to feel comfortable" identifying herself as "biracial."

Another important component of Catherine's cultural identity is that she converted to Judaism, the faith of her husband, Simon. After attending services at several synagogues in the Boston area, Catherine and her family have joined a liberal suburban congregation. They feel comfortable in this congregation, which is "open to a lot of different people."

Catherine and Simon married while they were in college. Today they are both practicing lawyers living in a Boston suburb with a strong public school system. The school where their older daughter is a third-grader is very ethnically diverse, with thirty-three different languages spoken in students' homes.

For Catherine skin color differences are paramount in defining racial identification and experience. As a child, her light skin was both valued by her darker adoptive parents and devalued by her peers. She believes that had she been darker, her adoptive parents would not have wanted to adopt her: "Complexion was very important to my adopted mother. The color issue was very important to her, so that always made me feel nervous—anxious about complexion." Her peers, however, sometimes belittled her for her light skin color, making it impossible for her to discuss her concerns about racial identity with them. Moreover, since her adoptive mother was not nurturing and her other older relatives were not warm with her, Catherine was unable to discuss her racial identity concerns with anyone.

At birth, Catherine's older daughter had blond hair and blue eyes. As a parent of a child who is white in appearance, Catherine's great fear has been that others would not perceive her relationship with her child. Her maternal relationship, in fact, has been challenged more than once. At the time of her daughter's birth, when a nurse brought the baby to Catherine in the hospital, "there was a little bit of a mix-up. The nurse said, 'Oh, no, this is the wrong baby.' It was just my fear of what would happen—that people would not think that we were together." A few years later, a daycare provider did not recognize Catherine as her daughter's mother, and a Hebrew teacher did not make the relational connection between Catherine and her child. In Catherine's experience, only white people fail to perceive the mother-child relationship between Catherine and her daughter: "If caregivers are people of color, that doesn't happen."

In order to rear biracial children Catherine considers that it is imperative to expose them to "people of similar backgrounds." Toward that end her family has joined both a multiracial family organization and a multiracial Jewish family network. The latter includes not only people of color but white non-Jews. The godparents for Catherine's older daughter are Jewish and for her second daughter they are a biracial couple. Since Catherine's parents have died and Simon's live in Chicago, Catherine perceives the importance of close friends who share the biracial reality of her family.

Catherine is keenly aware of the different kinds of experience that her children have in public places when they are alone with their white father and when they are with her. When they are with him, they are assumed to be white; when they are with her, she and they may experience hyper-surveillance. She described an incident in Bloomingdale's where a security person followed her and her daughter. She also mentioned that she is very careful about handling her purchases in stores. She has told her daughter, "Mommy will always want a bag, because they will immediately think that Mommy is taking it without paying for it. So when I go to the store, if I'm carrying something, I'll carry it further out, rather than carrying merchandise close before I pay for it."

Nevertheless, Simon's and the children's perceived whiteness can lead to challenges of the appropriateness of their presence in certain settings. Catherine's older daughter was challenged when she joined the "Affinity Group" for African American students in her school until she recounted the Bloomingdale's surveillance incident: "She told the kids that we were being watched in Bloomingdale's because of race and she felt proud in telling that story, because the kids in the group immediately could identify with that—'Oh, yeah, we've been watched, too.'" Similarly, when Simon and the children are alone at a multiracial family group event, they will be asked, "And why are you here?"

As a parent who has confronted conundrums of color throughout her life, Catherine seeks to ensure that her daughters will feel more comfortable with their biraciality than she. Of her older daughter, Catherine says, "I don't know that I'd say she's comfortable with it, but she doesn't struggle with it as I did." Catherine and her husband, therefore, have sought to expose their children to people like themselves—who are biracial and who are Jewish.

Adopted and biracial herself, Catherine's relationship to her older daughter was questioned from birth, probably increasing the sense of trauma usually associated with the event. Catherine has had a lingering apprehension under different circumstances about being asked, "Is that your child?" She, her husband, and children belong to family organizations that offer social contacts with other multiracial families to validate the biracial reality of their family. Aware of perceptions of their family composition in public places, she also brings to the attention of her daughters how they sometimes are under surveillance in commercial settings, a situation one of her daughters described to a peer group that questioned her racial authenticity.

EUROPEAN AMERICAN MOTHERS

Profile 10: Ruth and Her Son and Daughter

Ruth, who is white, has been married to Augustus, a lawyer, for thirty-four years. Their son, a graduate of an Ivy-league college, is twenty-seven years old; their daughter, aged twenty, is currently an Ivy-league college student. Ruth regards her children as "multiracial," although she said they consider themselves "black and Jewish." She said, "We've raised our kids as Jewish," and "my husband really is more responsible for their black identity than I am." Their "multiracial" experiences are associated with her husband's family, particularly his mother, who spent her last years in their Victorian Brookline home in a neighborhood that is "principally white."

In their public elementary school years, her son developed an enduring friendship with another biracial boy. She could not recall his reporting an incident relating to race. Her daughter, however, had painful experiences with feeling "different." Her hair was an issue. There were no other black girls in her class. Ruth recalled an incident initiated by a white girl's refusal to play with "black girls." Ruth and her husband met with the principal, teachers, and the parents, who expressed remorse. To afford their daughter multiracial contacts, they chose summer camps where she had "an opportunity to branch out" in a more diverse environment. At "fabulous" Brookline High School, she flourished; there she was able "to put her [elementary] school experience behind her." They selected a private boy's school for their son, because they had heard Brookline High was not a good place for black boys.

While their children enjoy close relationships with their father's Virginia-based family and friends, there is "less of a relationship" between her family and her children, who are aware that Ruth's parents opposed the marriage. She said that "on the surface" there was peace when their respective families came together around holiday events and family celebrations, as when their children were bar/bat mitzvahed.

Their circle of friends is more white than black, and some of their friends are "involved in interracial relationships." She remarked, "There hasn't been a total acceptance of us in black circles," and related that her attending a Jack and Jill event had been discouraged.

With regard to satisfaction with her childrearing, Ruth said, "Our kids feel very comfortable in both worlds that Augustus and I have brought to our marriage. . . . My heritage has always been very important to me and the fact that I was able to transmit that to my children with Augustus's total consent and support and involvement is very important to me and my children." She continues to regret that growing up in the Boston area, they had little exposure to black and other multiracial kids.

A key consideration in their childrearing has been giving their children a global perspective through international travel. Another has been being open and able to talk about issues with their children. Augustus has been a loving, involved father; he's been very involved in the community; he's been a good role model, she said. She added that he made the choice about where to live and where to rear their kids.

In their family, Jewish identity is as important as racial identity, the former buttressed by the composition of the neighborhood and schools as well as religious practice, and the latter by their sturdy paternal African American family heritage. The difference in the early peer relations of their son and daughter points to the intersection of gender and biracial/racial incidents. Through summers in a multiracial camp and international travel, Ruth and her husband have tried to compensate for their children's limited exposure to black and other biracial children. Ruth regrets bringing them up in a principally white context.

Profile 11: Beatrice and Her Two Daughters and Son

Beatrice is a fifty-nine-year-old white mother of three, two daughters and a son. Trained as an interior designer and artist, she recalled an encounter with a teacher who asked her how old her children were when she adopted them. Taken aback, she said, "Almost immediately when I saw them after I gave birth." She added the teacher "couldn't see past the color." On another occasion, her children's pediatrician inquired about "her experience with color." Misunderstanding his question—as an artist, she assumed he was asking about "color, hues, tints"—she belatedly realized that he was referring to race. Her response finally was, "I really can't tell you that. I'm just the mother of my kids."

If her "kids," now between twenty and twenty-seven years of age, had problems or issues related to race, Beatrice said they brought them to her "well after the fact." Issues of race, she said, "may have been fielded" more by her husband than by her. She admitted that her daughters suffered teasing because of their curly hair.

She suggested that race has not been salient in her parenting experience. She said: "Race is something we almost never talk about within this house." She credits the private schools and colleges her children have attended with giving them "a forum, a format and vocabulary, and a safe community" for shaping their self-perceptions with respect to race. For one year, her eldest child, a daughter named Faith, attended a public school where she encountered difficult situations. According to Beatrice, her daughter never related the difficulties in terms of race.

For more than thirty years, Beatrice and her family have lived in a section of Boston's Dorchester neighborhood during a phase of neighborhood transition from Irish to African American. The decision to live in Dorchester was hers; she recalled her husband's saying, "I've been living in a white world all my life; I don't care where we live." She made an effort to involve her children in cultural experiences in the community. For example, she facilitated their participation in *Black Nativity*, a decision "driven by keeping my children in a world where they might not be the only ones."

Vacations and visits with Beatrice's family in Spofford, New Hampshire, exposed her children to the realm of privilege in which she herself had grown up. They joined the Lake Club in Spofford, where her children made friends—friendships, she said, her children keep up with. Faith, who is married, lives in a New Hampshire town. Her son lives in New York City. Her youngest, a daughter, is in college in Ohio.

Having grown up with little contact with blacks except as family servants, Beatrice's marriage to Jack was in the spirit of rebellion. She spoke of her father's displeasure at the time they were wed. Her children have been "embraced by" her family and have close ties to some of their cousins. There was little reference to the role of her husband's family, based in Florida, in their upbringing. She simply stated: "I feel totally comfortable going anywhere in my family as a family or going anywhere in his family as a family—and they are two really different places."

With regard to important considerations in rearing their children, Beatrice said that the involvement of a nurturing father was essential and that regarding themselves as a family and not as a social experiment was also important.

Beatrice's narrative presents some contradictions. While attempting to ignore or transcend the relevance of race, she and her husband made a residential choice that afforded contact with black and white neighbors. They subscribed to multicultural and predominately African American cultural activities, suggesting an interest in strengthening a sense of biracial identity in their offspring. The insulation that comes with white privilege allows Beatrice to overlook societal responses to race, and perhaps discourages open discussion of race-related matters until "well after the fact."

Profile 12: Joan and Her Six Children

In her mid-sixties, Joan looks back on her experiences in the 1960s as the young mother of six biracial children born between 1963 and 1971. Joan and her African American husband were community activists living in a town south of Boston; they participated in fair housing efforts, she was a town meeting member, they marched for civil rights and for peace. Yet she felt isolated by her maternal responsibilities, her lack of extended family support, and her husband's absences for work and for community activities. To increase her connectedness to others, she helped to found a food co-op and had a shared babysitting arrangement with two other families. Nevertheless, she did not know anyone who shared her experience of biracial parenting.

She described her identification with the author of *Beyond the Whiteness of Whiteness*.[2]

I very much identified with the author, who is white and who talks about having given birth to children of color. You are a different person or she [the author] felt that way. The way she talks about it is the way I feel. I'm sure my friends have no sense of that and live in a different world. I feel that my world is different. It may not always look so from the outside, the way I view the world, the way I view myself. The way I have endured in a sense. I've been through some unpleasant experiences. Rejection—that type of thing. Made to feel less or people trying to make you feel that way because of who you are and this is your family. You never can go back. I've learned so much. I've been very much opened up in my professional life [as a registered nurse], very much focused on multicultural issues. I'm still involved in opening that up; I'm not sure that I would have been open to those experiences in the same way [if I had not had biracial children].

When Joan and her husband married in 1962, none of their parents attended their wedding. Although her parents became reconciled to her marriage with the birth of her eldest son, her mother-in-law was never close to Joan's children. She was more concerned with helping a daughter with her large family. Joan's husband's and her circle of friends included black and white families, though she does not recall that any of them were particularly involved with discussing racial identity issues with the children.

Acknowledging that parenting is a challenging experience for which most people are unprepared, Joan feels fortunate that her nursing education had involved many child psychology courses. "I think you have to let children know how valued they are. If I were starting out now, I would try to balance" the two identities more. Joan and her husband had anticipated that their children would have an African American identity and they had promoted that by discussing color differences and by exposing them to black cultural experiences. But in the 1960s and 1970s, "We felt that because of where we were living, because of the politics that they really had to know of their blackness."

Although Joan's children are fair-skinned, they are visually identifiable as people of color. While they were growing up, the girls were very active in school sports and student government, though rarely dating. Her sons encountered some difficulties with peers around racial issues. Joan recalls that her children chose their friends carefully. Today they are all successful professionals—working in academia, in the business world, and in law.

Looking back Joan is proud of her accomplishments as a parent but wishes that she had provided more support for herself when her children were young: "I am the person I am because of my marriage and my motherhood, and that's related to the fact that I am the mother of biracial children."

Rejected by her own family-of-origin and her husband's African American relatives, with six children born in a span of eight years, Joan felt extremely isolated in a white ethnic suburb south of Boston. Although active in community work and a participant in a shared babysitting arrangement, she did not know anyone else with biracial children. She and her husband discussed racial differences and exposed their children to African American cultural experiences. Despite lacking social and emotional support during her childrearing years, Joan regards the outcome with pride and satisfaction.

Profile 13: Debby, Her Sons, and Her Stepdaughter

Fifty-four-year-old Debby is the mother of two sons who are aged thirty-three and thirty-two. She also has a thirty-three-year-old stepdaughter. Married twice, both husbands African American, Debby is white. She grew up in New Jersey with a father whose national background was English and Irish and a mother of Polish descent. Estranged from her family-of-origin "because of the race issue," she feels that her mother's racism was instrumental in keeping her apart from other relatives.

In 1972, Debby moved from New Jersey to join Lester in the Dorchester section of Boston. Their first son was born in Boston at a time when school busing had heightened racial tensions in the city. A second son was born a year later. Disowned by her family, with no relatives or friends in Boston, and a husband who "wasn't very supportive," Debby was extremely isolated. Trained in nursing, she worked evenings in a Boston hospital where the schedule—ten days on and four days off—undermined domestic life.

When her older son was two-and-a-half and the other a year younger, Debby's relationship with Lester faltered. She left him, moving to Boston's multiethnic South End where she lived with her sons until 1981. A single mother, she relied on a daycare center for childcare: "It enabled me to go back to work and for the children to be safe; and we had friends—we met people and we had a social life." Debby met Luke, who had a daughter, Sheila, who was "very needy." She found herself with a biracial stepdaughter as well as two biracial sons.

When she and Luke met, they shared several common attributes: they were single parents, both had racially mixed children, and both were Catholic. Over the years, with the decline in church programs and their move to another neighborhood, they lost their "sense of church"—an identity with the church. In recent years, Debby has returned to the church, while Luke has started meditating and exploring unorganized religion.

Despite having three kids "with varied schedules," she went back to school and obtained a paralegal certificate and a bachelor's degree. By that time, her sons were attending a parochial school that was racially mixed. Her stepdaughter was enrolled in a private school where there was little support for her racial identity and where social class issues were as difficult for her as racial issues. Debby said that seven-year-old Sheila "was having problems in school with kids" and sought a black psychotherapist to aid her. The therapist suggested that Sheila needed a relationship with her birth mother, who declined committing to a relationship.

Debby tried to help Sheila by increasing her exposure to "multicultural" situations and encouraging contacts with "multiracial friends." She invited black and multiracial children for sleepovers and sent Sheila to summer camp where children were predominately African American. She wanted to ensure the presence of positive African American role models in her life. Debby's sons went to an "all brown" summer camp, where campers and counselors were mostly black and brown (Hispanic). She mentioned vacations with the children in settings where races mixed with ease and eight trips to Jamaica to expose them to a country with a different racial composition and "different socioeconomics."

As they advanced in school, Debby's sons moved from the Catholic school to a Boston public school and then to a public school in suburban Natick, Massachusetts, to which they were bussed under the auspices of METCO. She said with pride that she was "born an advocate." To promote what was in the best interests of her sons in the suburban school, Debby became involved in Natick's school issues and events. Her sons were active in school programs and sports. They had solid friendships with Natick classmates and their families. Samuel, the older son, was captain of the football team in his senior year and the first METCO president of a senior class: "Samuel had so much going on in the suburbs; I think that's why he married a Natick girl and lives in Natick now. And he was out there a lot more than Craig was."

Craig had two sets of friends, his Natick friends and his Boston friends, and a dual identity. Debby describes him as "the kid who would go to the suburbs and be what they wanted him to be; and he was the kid who could ride home on the bus and get off the bus and be who he needed to be." She added, "Craig and Sheila teased Samuel at times about his racial identity and who he felt identified with. Now they wouldn't do that, because Samuel presents as a strong black male."

Debby cited incidents in which her being white was an issue with regard to her children. She was challenged by a parent who charged that since Debby is white, her sons did not need the advantage of suburban schooling through the METCO program. Her retort was that her children were brown and that she was white "wasn't going to change their face to society or their opportunities in the world. I was trying to maximize everything for them." At a school conference on tutoring at Sheila's middle school, parents were divided by racial groups, black parents assigned to one room and white parents to another. When she accompanied Luke to the room designated for black parents, Debby was confronted by school personnel who insisted that she belonged in the other room. After a protracted debate, she persuaded them that she should be with her husband, because they were there to talk about their daughter and her requirements. On a pre-college tour, Debby visited Washington, D.C., institutions with Sheila. She recalled: "There have been very few times, but that was one of the times that I felt uncomfortable—walking around the Howard campus with Sheila. I felt very conspicuous and very I don't belong here. And does my daughter belong here? What would it be like visiting her afterwards? And she did go to Howard." Samuel went to Northeastern University in Boston and Craig chose a historically black college, Johnson C. Smith in South Carolina.

Appraising her role as mother and stepmother, Debby said, "I think I gave them all I could give in terms of who they were. . . . I wish I could have given them more of my family." Her aunt and uncle, a nun and a priest, became involved in their lives and visited frequently. When her mother died, Debby's relatives started visiting. She said that they've "been accepted" by her father's side of the family, but not by her mother's side.

The family of Debby's first husband, the father of her sons, has been close and supportive. She felt it was very important for her children to have grandparents, aunts, and uncles who reinforced their racial identity. She herself made an effort to maintain contact with them.

As for her parenting, Debby reported with pride and satisfaction on the professional work of her offspring: Samuel is starting an executive detection security business; Craig is program director in a facility for homeless children; and Sheila is embarking with fellowship support on a graduate program in creative writing. Both sons have white wives and Sheila has a live-in boyfriend.

Debby, a vigorous advocate for her sons and stepdaughter, responded directly when challenged about their requirements and her role and relationship in their lives. There is evidence of courage and tenacity in her account, and initiative in seeking multicultural settings for the children. In addition to relatives, a priest and a nun, who have taken an interest in Debby's household, belatedly others—previously estranged—have begun to visit them. Still, she feels that earlier acquaintance with her family background would have contributed to her sons' identity formation.

Profile 14: Celeste and Her Daughter

Celeste, who is white, and her husband, Dick, both hold doctorates with a concentration in African American history. They bring to childrearing an interest in advancing the African American dimensions of their offspring's experience. Their only child is an eight-year-old daughter, Maya. Maya understands that she is biracial. Celeste reported that Maya was proud of being biracial. She has been told she is biracial rather than African American; however, if she looked different, "it might be a different story." She is fair-skinned with corkscrew curly light brown hair. Celeste stated that Maya probably did not understand race as a concept at all. While she appeared shocked when hearing about slavery, Maya has not yet understood the potential relevance of race in her future. Celeste stated that "because of the neighborhood we live in and the school she goes to," race is not a problem. Maya attends a charter school where she has had a Chinese American kindergarten teacher and, in first grade, an African American teacher.

Hair, however, is a problem. Maya wouldn't let Celeste comb her hair. When the school nurse had to comb Maya's hair, Celeste felt humiliated. It wasn't a "race thing," but

Celeste saw it in racial terms. She felt school personnel would wonder: "What kind of mother is she that she can't comb her child's hair?" Advised about hair products and referred to African American hairdressers, Celeste—and Maya—have dealt with their hair problems. Celeste concluded: "The hair is the bane of my existence."

With regard to family relationships that may influence Maya's racial development, Celeste acknowledged that colleagues and friends serve as surrogate family. Celeste's mother was "very unhappy" about the marriage, as were Celeste's siblings. Her mother has never visited them, although they travel to Ohio to visit her. She loves Maya and has come to accept Dick. Dick's family, on the other hand, was described as "welcoming and wonderful." They hold family reunions in Florida that they have attended with Maya. There are other interracial marriages in Dick's family—cousins with children.

The intellectual commitment to African American history on the part of Celeste and her husband ensures exposure to situations that reinforce Maya's future comprehension of the relevance of race. Their choice of a multicultural neighborhood and school environment should foster Maya's sense of belonging. Celeste, like many other white mothers of biracial daughters, attempts to cope with the texture and appearance of Maya's hair.

Celeste's mother, over the years, seems to recognize—if not fully accept—her marital choice. Relative estrangement from her family contrasts keenly with the embrace extended by her husband's family. The disparity is likely to tilt Maya's identification toward her African American heritage.

Profile 15: Joanna and Her Son

Joanna, a white social worker and area manager in a child protective office, is the single mother of an eight-year-old son, Timothy, whom she describes as black or African American. They live in Boston's Roxbury area.

Joanna reported that Timothy sometimes asks, "Why are you white? My skin's brown." She tells him that he is a mix between his father's skin color and her skin color. She admits that it is "very difficult," because Timothy doesn't have a relationship with his father. "I feel so badly for him that he doesn't know his father. . . . He just went off the deep end and disappeared." She has no contact with his father's family, immigrants from Barbados. She has told Timothy a little about Barbados and that people came from Africa to Barbados. She thinks he is beginning to understand, but does not yet have "an emotional piece" tied to whatever he comprehends. "I'm sure it's very difficult for him to not know his father," she adds.

Joanna's relatives are present in their lives. Her nieces attend programs at Timothy's school. Her brother and sister-in-law take him on adventure trips and skiing in Maine where she is certain he is "probably the only person of color." He had two daycare providers, both African American, before going to school. In the daycare settings, the children were African American and Latino, a mix of races and cultures. A frequent user of the Roxbury YMCA,

Joanna is often the only white person she sees there when accompanying Timothy. Neither she nor Timothy has had a race-related encounter there.

In public places, however, people sometimes speak to Timothy in Spanish. He has asked why; she explained that perhaps he looks like he is Spanish-speaking. He sometimes pretends that he speaks Spanish.

For Joanna, an important consideration in her relationship with her son is being authentic, faithful to who she is, or, as she put it, "I just try to be myself." By that she means she tries to find answers to difficult questions and she makes an effort to expose him to "every kind of difference in the world."

In her capacity as a social worker, Joanna does emergency foster care for a hotline. This is another source of contacts with youths from different backgrounds who sometimes spend a night or two in their home.

Timothy attends a church-affiliated school in Roxbury, founded expressly for African American children. She feels it is a school where they have only high expectations for pupils, with a "mix of old-fashioned academic training" and cultural and spiritual education. Having considered opportunities in suburban schools associated with METCO, she decided she did not want to send him on a bus to diversify a school community in which he does not live. The problematic experience she has had at his school is when "people sometimes get confused about who I am to him."

Joanna mentioned the many ways in which she has tried to ensure Timothy's exposure to African American cultural events and racially mixed settings. He has been to a YMCA summer camp and participated in other summer programs that have racially diverse participants. She said she has a diverse group of friends, so she thinks "he manages not to feel that he's in two different worlds. It's like one big world that's not racially segregated in any kind of way."

As for the future she envisions for Timothy, Joanna said, "A lot of times he's said he wants to be a teacher. . . . He's really good with science and math. I would want him to just be happy and comfortable with himself and have good, healthy, supportive friendships. And after that he probably can do anything."

This single white mother of a young son has made a residential choice that probably provides a "comfort zone" for them. At his Afrocentric school, however, Joanna is not readily identified as his mother. And in some situations, Timothy is taken to be Hispanic. Through his exposure to racially mixed settings, she hopes he will now experience a racially integrated dimension of society. She brings to childrearing some features of her professional experience as a social worker. Although she regrets the lack of the presence of Timothy's father and his family in their lives, she is grateful for her relatives' involvement.

SUMMARY

We crafted these profiles to illuminate compelling aspects of individual mothers' experiences. Common threads, however, run throughout these profiles. Maintaining contacts with relatives or becoming reconciled to severed family relations, confronting color conundrums, and being challenged about relationships with their children are a few examples of themes that mothers of biracial children express across generations and racial lines.

NOTES

1. Jack and Jill of America, Inc., was founded in Philadelphia in 1938 "with the idea of bringing together [middle- and upper-middle-class African American] children in a social and cultural environment." It has grown into a national organization with chapters across the country and collaborative relations with the Links and the Children's Defense Foundation.

2. Jane Lazarre, *Beyond the Whiteness of Whiteness: Memoir of a White Mother of Black Sons* (Durham, N.C.: Duke University Press, 1996).

4

Nurturing Biracial Children: Some Lessons Learned

You've got to believe that the world is good enough to receive them and that they will make it the beloved kingdom that [Martin Luther] King talked about. You've got to believe that.

The biracial parenting experiences of the mothers with whom we talked span a half-century. While certain common challenges occurred across the generations, major changes in U.S. society have affected the parenting experiences of mothers nurturing biracial children today. Our conversations about confronting the challenges and rewards of parenting biracial children suggest positive strategies that we believe other parents of biracial children may find useful.

IDENTITY AND IDENTIFICATION

Mothers of younger and older biracial children cite the challenges presented by their children's ambiguous racial identity and its implications. For most mothers the question of how their offspring regarded themselves racially was complicated. Some had prenatal expectations about the racial identity of their children, usually assuming they would be biracial or African American in appearance. To be sure, there were a few genetic surprises for mothers, black and white, who had Caucasian-looking offspring. In families with more than one child, variations in children's racial characteristics presented a challenge and a chance to consider differences in cultural responses to individuals determined by racial characteristics, such as skin color, hair texture, and other physical features.

Allowing children to define who they are very early "so that they can inform you of how they are receiving the world" requires close monitoring of expressions of self-awareness and definition. In other words, it is important to make an effort "to ensure they have their own identity before they have a racial identity; and to ensure they understand they are a mixture of both races." Studies of racial awareness report evidence of ability to recognize and verbalize racial characteristics and differences occurs between three to five years of age. By the time children are in kindergarten or first grade, they are likely to have an awareness of how they are perceived racially. They begin to label themselves and others in terms of racial characteristics.

As they develop, children are exposed to race-related contacts, comments, and conversations; the content of television, film, and print material are other sources of cultural messages about the relevance of race. It is then—in the middle years—that the dialogue with parents about race assumes enormous importance. Retrospectively, several mothers regretted that they had missed or avoided occasions to explore references to race with their children. In some instances, mothers only learned years later of racially charged situations their offspring had encountered.

Toward fostering a positive view of self with regard to race, our conversations with mothers across the generations suggest the following positive strategies:

- Create a climate for open discussion of race and race-related matters;
- Talk about your own history and experiences with respect to race;
- Elicit conversations that involve mutual self-examination;
- Attempt to reconcile differences with relatives who oppose interracial relationships and reject biracial children;
- Promote children's appreciation of their racial heritages;
- Facilitate associations with black and white relatives;
- Instill a sense of pride in being biracial.

TRANSGENERATIONAL BIRACIAL PARENTING CHALLENGES

Since mothers and their biracial children usually have different skin tones, many strangers fail to perceive the relationship between them. European Americans—more often than Americans of color—do not see other more subtle physical clues to their relationships, such as facial features, body carriage, or gestures. Indeed, the pervasive query, "Is that your child?" in the presence of one's off-spring is an example of public intrusiveness that calls for affirmative parental response. It is likely that the setting in which the question is posed does not afford the chance to explore the questioner's curiosity. Only later, one formulates what one might have said: "Why do you ask?" "What did you think when you looked at us?" The denial or questioning of the relationship between mother and child represents one of the most painful challenges of biracial parenting for mothers across the generations.

Most mothers, white and black, acknowledged the need for vigilance—protective and defensive—in the early years of childrearing. They anticipated the day when their daughters and sons would be confronted by peers or adults who questioned or denigrated their appearance, family composition, and, more profoundly, identity. Black mothers, recalling racist encounters in their youth, wanted to equip their children (especially those African American in appearance) with emotional and verbal responses to offensive criticism and harassment. Several white mothers anticipated incidents and prepared their children with examples of retorts.

Often the need for guidance and advice about dealing with situations was recognized only after a problem occurred or a racist attack had happened. Initially, race-related situations arise in the early years at school or in the neighborhood. Name-calling, that is, being the object of the "n" word, derisive names for physical features—especially hair—bullying, and excluding their children from groups or events created moments for maternal introspection, intervention, and sometimes action. Helping children to counteract these emotionally difficult situations is a persistent challenge for mothers of biracial children.

In adolescence, incidents also occurred in commercial settings where blacks are frequently targets of hyper-surveillance. Boys report these experiences more frequently than girls. Mothers also reported more subtle social snubs or slights and deliberate attempts to exclude or diminish the presence of their visibly African American children.

When children are young, the demonstration of maternal concern about negative incidents is important to building confidence and evidence of support for the desire for fair play and equal treatment. When such episodes occur, some useful intervention strategies include:

- Listen closely and sympathetically to the child's account of the incident; determine who was involved and who witnessed the situation;
- Give the child a notion of what you plan to do with regard to the episode;
- At the earliest feasible time, bring the incident to the attention of the adult(s) with authority (e.g., teacher, school principal, store manager) in the situation and engage them in a discussion of the matter;

- Try to reach agreement on what action will follow to influence behavior, interaction, policy, or practice;
- Inform the child of your action on his or her behalf and suggest what she or he should do if a similar incident happens in the future.

SOCIOCULTURAL CHANGE AND BIRACIAL PARENTING

Women rearing biracial children today do so in a sociocultural context that differs significantly from that of their mothers' generation. The increase in interracial marriages in recent decades has led to an increase in the number of biracial children. Although marriages between blacks and whites are fewer than between other racial groups, they are significantly greater than thirty or forty years ago.[1] Associated with the increased number of racially ambiguous Americans are increased resources and supports for biracial parenting. Today websites and journals deal with issues of multiracial parenting; more books affirm multiracial identities for young children; more multicultural events are available for biracial children to attend; more images of biracial children and adults appear in newspapers, in popular magazines, and on television; and books are available that explore biraciality not only from social science perspectives but also from those of personal experience. Thus, there is more cultural support for mothers of biracial children today and there is greater awareness of biraciality in American society than a generation ago.

One of the consequences of this increased awareness of biraciality is that biracial children have the opportunity to affirm publicly their multiple racial identities. They can tell the world that they are African American and Scottish; that they are white and black; that they are biracial. Their mothers can hope that as adults they will claim all their racial heritages and not simply their African American heritage, as American society dictated in the past.

Nevertheless, while today there are more social and cultural supports for biracial parenting and for acknowledging diverse racial heritages, racism is still pervasive in American society. Biracial children encounter racial slurs from their playmates; biracial children experience hyper-surveillance in stores and other public places; biracial children may confront low expectations of academic performance from teachers. Mothers of today's biracial children still need to be vigilant as they prepare their children to face confidently a world that is not always welcoming of them.

Our conversations with mothers of biracial children of different generations revealed several positive parenting strategies for nurturing and preparing biracial children to engage confidently with the world outside their homes. Four of the most salient of these strategies are:

- Ensure that biracial children appreciate their dual heritages;
- Encourage dialogue around racial matters;
- Expose biracial children to people like themselves; and
- Advocate for one's children.

While these strategies can be useful for mothers of all children, they have a special importance among biracial children.

Ensuring that biracial children are aware of their dual heritages provides them with a foundation for self-confidence about their racial identity. Some of the ways that mothers reported for developing this awareness included not only interactions with extended family members and discussion of parents' personal backgrounds but also illustrations of family history in photographs. Works of African American and European American artists in their homes and attendance at cultural events expose children to the arts and intellectual gifts of both heritages. Such activities encourage children to appreciate their rich family heritages and the diverse and significant contributions that African Americans and European Americans have made to society in the United States.

Encouraging dialogue around racial matters enables children and parents to share problematic experiences. Several mothers stressed the importance of listening to children and learning from them about issues in their lives. Maintaining such dialogue is more difficult as children mature and begin to encounter issues that accompany adolescence, but an early foundation of openness and exchange enhances the likelihood of discussing problematic racial experiences later. Nevertheless, almost all mothers mentioned that they often did not learn of painful childhood racial encounters for many years.

Exposing biracial children to children like themselves enables children to enhance a sense of comfort about their biraciality. Mothers parenting children today frequently mentioned the choice of a multiracial neighborhood as desirable, though they did not always live in such a neighborhood. Some mothers of adult biracial offspring regretted not having provided their children with such neighborhoods. Most mothers—whether of younger or adult biracial offspring—mentioned the importance of friendships with other biracial families throughout their children's growing-up years. In addition, many mothers spoke of the choices of schools, camps, and cultural activities as being influenced by their multiracial and multiethnic composition. Underlying the provision of such opportunities for exposure to and interaction with other biracial people is the belief that children will feel more comfortable about their racial identities and their biracial families when they know that many other people are like them.

Advocating for biracial children on racial matters is an important parenting strategy. When mothers respond courteously but forcefully to incidents of racial stereotyping, they model a valuable coping strategy for their children. If the relationship between a mother and her biracial child is challenged, the mother's affirmation of the relationship sends an important message to her child as well as to the challenger. Some mothers stressed the importance of responding to negative racial encounters when and wherever they occur. Such negative experiences, of course, provide parents and children with opportunities for dialogue about the incidents.

A retrospective view of social conventions and cultural milieu in the United States in the latter half of the twentieth century elicits admiration for the courage of interracial couples who entered into marriage and parenting in that era. Older mothers, black and white, experienced a sense of singularity and sometimes isolation in their residential settings. For their generation, neighborhood and school choices in the Boston area were limited. The chance of encountering other families with biracial children was slim. Schools with "rainbow" enrollments did not exist.

The trend toward less contentious race relations affords different and improved conditions for rearing biracial children in the twenty-first century. What we learned from younger mothers about the choice of social contexts and cultural influences is instructive for the future:

- Select multiracial and multicultural neighborhoods and schools to reinforce values related to biracial family life;
- Participate in activities and events that involve people of varied racial and cultural backgrounds;
- Make use of books, films, videos, exhibitions, and other media that offer affirming content;
- Monitor the print media, televised programs, and other electronic media for content that undermines the status of biracial individuals; make known to your offspring what programs or materials are objectionable and why;

- Cultivate an interest in other cultures and countries through books, museum visits, other media, and travel, if possible.

CONCLUSION

Being the mother of a biracial child adds a dimension to parenting that mothers of monoracial children do not share. Preparing one's children to be confident about their biraciality in a society that does not always recognize or welcome biraciality is the challenge that all mothers of biracial children confront. There are unique rewards as well as challenges that such mothers experience. Here we have suggested some of the strategies that we think foster successful biracial parenting.

We learned that success in rearing biracial children requires involvement with other people—relatives, neighbors, friends, teachers, playmates, and classmates—of different racial and cultural backgrounds. That today it is more acceptable—indeed, sometimes ostensibly fashionable—to be biracial does not mean such individuals will be spared the curiosity, envy, or contempt of a few. What we have learned from mothers of biracial children has given us insight into circumstance and treatment in the recent past. We urge more comprehensive studies of experiences of and with biracial offspring that explore the relevance of regional conventions, social class, religious orientations, and varied biracial combinations. The experiences and opinions of fathers are needed to understand fully the dynamics of biracial families. The pursuit of such projects is essential, for biracial individuals are the population of the future.

NOTE

1. See Appendix I.

Appendix I

Interracial Marriages in the United States[1]

Year	Black/White Marriages	Black Husband White Wife	Black Wife White Husband
1960	51,000	25,000	26,000
1970	65,000	41,000	24,000
1980	121,000	94,000	27,000
1990	213,000	159,000	54,000
2000	335,308	239,477	95,831
2006	403,000	286,000	117,000

1. The 1967 Supreme Court decision in *Loving v. Virginia* legalized interracial marriages in the United States. Data in Appendix I are from the U.S. Census. The AARP reported that its 2004 survey showed 70 percent whites and 80 percent blacks approved of interracial marriages between blacks and whites—only 4 percent whites approved in 1958 (*AARP The Magazine* (May and June 2004), 45–46).

Appendix II

Some Sociological Attributes of Mothers

Race	Education	Occupation	Marital Status	Residence	Children's Status
Black	JD	Professor	Married	Urban	2 adults
White	BFA	Consultant	Married	Urban	3 adults
White	MCP	Administrator Nonprofit	Married	Suburban	2 adults
White	BS	University Lecturer	Married**	Urban	3 adults
Black	PhD	University Administrator*	Married**	Urban	1 adult
Black	BM	University Administrator*	Married	Urban	1 adult
Black	BSN	Consultant	Married	Urban	2 adults
White	PhD	Professor	Married**	Urban	2 adults
White	MSN	Nurse	Divorced	Urban	6 adults
White	PhD	University Administrator*	Married	Suburban	3 adults
Black	JD	Attorney	Married	Suburban	2 children
Black	JD	Attorney	Married	Urban	1 child
Black	JD	Professor	Married	Urban	1 child
Black	PhD	Professor	Divorced	Urban	1 child
Black	BA	Consultant	Married**	Urban	1 adult and 1 child
White	MSW	Administrator	Single	Urban	1 child
Black	MA	Homemaker	Married	Suburban	3 children
Black	BA	Administrator Nonprofit	Married	Suburban	1 child
Black	JD	Attorney	Married	Urban	2 children
White	PhD	Administrator Nonprofit	Married	Urban	1 child
White	High School	Consultant	Married	Rural	3 adults and 1 child

Key:
* retired
** current marriage is second or third

Appendix III

Selected Multiracial Resources

Association of Multiethnic Americans, Inc.
Nationwide organization in the United States with affiliates across the country
P.O. Box 29223, Los Angeles, CA 90029-0223
www.amesite.org

Cookies and Cream Website: Biracial and Multicultural Organizations, E-zines, Groups, and other links
www.cookiesandcreamteam.com

Dolls Like Me
Website with resources on building self-esteem in children of color
www.dollslikeme.com

MAVIN Foundation
Publishes MAVIN magazine and Multicultural Child Re-
source Book
www.mavinfoundation.org

My Shoes
Web-based support group for multiracial people who have
a white phenotype
www.myshoes.com

National Advocacy for the Multi-Ethnic (N.A.M.E.)
www.namecentral.org

Selected References

Cross, June. *Secret Daughter: A Mixed-Race Daughter and the Mother Who Gave Her Away.* New York: Viking Penguin, Penguin Group USA, Inc., 2006.

Frankenberg, Ruth. *White Women, Race Matters: The Social Construction of Whiteness.* Minneapolis: University of Minnesota Press, 1993.

Funderberg, Lise. *Black, White, Other: Biracial Americans Talk About Racial Identity.* New York: William Morrow, 1994.

Gillespie, Peggy, and Gigi Kaesar. *Of Many Colors: Portraits of Multiracial Families.* Amherst: University of Massachusetts Press, 1994.

Kilson, Marion. *Claiming Place: Biracial Young Adults of the Post-Civil Rights Era.* Westport, Conn.: Bergin & Garvey, 2001.

Korgen, Kathleen Odell. *From Black to Biracial: Transforming Racial Identity Among Americans.* Westport, Conn.: Praeger Publishers, 1998.

Lazarre, Jane. *Beyond the Whiteness of Whiteness: Memoir of a White Mother of Black Sons.* Durham, N.C.: Duke University Press, 1996.

McBride, James. *The Color of Water: A Black Man's Tribute to His White Mother.* New York: Riverhead Books, 1996.

Nakazawa, Donna Jackson. *Does Anybody Else Look Like Me? A Parent's Guide to Raising Multiracial Children.* Cambridge, Mass.: Perseus Books, 2003.

Nissei, Angela. *Mixed: My Life in Black and White.* New York: Villard Books, Random House, 2006.

Obama, Barack. *Dreams from My Father: A Story of Race and Inheritance.* New York: Times Books, 1995.

O'Hearn, Claudine Chiawei, ed. *Half and Half: Writers on Growing Up Biracial and Bicultural.* New York: Pantheon Books, 1998.

Reddy, Maureen T. *Crossing the Color Line: Race, Parenting and Culture.* New Brunswick, N.J.: Rutgers University Press, 1994.

Root, Maria P. P., ed. *Racially Mixed People in America.* Newbury Park, Calif.: Sage Publications, 1992.

Rush, Sharon E. *Loving Across the Color Line: A White Adoptive Mother Learns About Race.* Lanham, Md.: Rowman & Littlefield Publishers, Inc., 2001.

Walker, Rebecca. *Black, White, and Jewish: Autobiography of a Shifting Self.* New York: Riverhead Books, Penguin Putnam, Inc., 2001.

Wright, Marguerite. *I'm Chocolate, You're Vanilla: Raising Healthy Black and Biracial Children in a Race-Conscious World.* New York: Jossey-Bass, 2000.

Index

About the Authors

Marion Kilson received her Ph.D. in social anthropology from Harvard University in 1967 and retired as dean of the graduate school at Salem State College in 2001. Her previous publications include *Claiming Place: Biracial Young Adults of the Post–Civil Rights Era* (Bergin and Garvey,

2001), three books on African topics, and many articles on African and African American society and culture. She and her husband live in Lexington, Massachusetts; their three children and six grandchildren live nearby in the Boston area.

Florence Ladd, psychologist and author, has taught at Simmons College and Harvard University and has held administrative positions at MIT, Wellesley College, and Radcliffe College, where she was director of the Bunting Institute. She authored the novel *Sarah's Psalm* (Scribner, 1996), and coauthored the book *Different Strokes* (Westview Press). Her essays are included in *A Stranger in the Village* (Griffin and Fish, eds.), *Grandmothers: Granddaughters Remember* (Marguerite Bouvard, ed.), *Dutiful Daughters* (Jean Gould, ed.), *Father* (Claudia O'Keefe, ed.), and *Rise Up Singing* (Cecelie Berry, ed.). She also contributed to *At Grandmother's Table* (Ellen Perry Berkeley, ed.). Her poems have appeared in *The Women's Review of Books, The Progressive, The Rockhurst Review,* and *Sweet Auburn.* She lives in Cambridge, Massachusetts.